21 Ways To Grow Your Business When The Going Gets Tough

David Madely

davidmadely.com

Table of Contents

INTRODUCTION

Steady Through the Storm – Why NOW is the Time to Ramp Up Your Marketing Efforts

When the economy slows, suddenly everything feels a little more uncertain. Budgets tighten, consumer confidence wobbles, and commerce braces for impact. It's during these times many small businesses instinctively pull back, tighten the purse strings, cut back and scale down their marketing efforts.

Big mistake!

This is exactly the time when you should NOT be cutting back on marketing and promoting your business. Challenging times are NOT the time to retreat – this is the time to regroup and *reimagine*.

You do not need to spend more money on marketing, you need to be *smarter* with how you market your business, be more *intentional* and laser-focused on what really works.

Whether it's nurturing the customers and clients who already love you, or streamlining your offerings to deliver absolute maximum value, you have all the tools at your finger tips to not only survive in tough times – but to truly thrive, leaving your competitors in the dust scratching their heads wondering what your secret is.

Well, your secret is right here, if – and ONLY if – you totally *commit to applying* the strategies in this book. Why? Because they work!

The marketing strategies and business growth methods I show you here are your secret weapon to weathering the storm; to rising above the uninspiring mediocrity you see everywhere.

Discover the most effective and proven marketing strategies that do not require big budgets or flashy and expensive advertising campaigns. Instead, they call for passion, ingenuity, adaptability, and a burning desire and willingness to get stuck in and demonstrate clearly what makes your business different... what makes it stand out head and shoulders above the crowd... what makes it the ONLY sensible option for people to choose.

People do not buy from just anyone. They buy from a business they trust; a business that exudes authenticity, authority, reliability, and real tangible value in bucket-loads. It's your job to demonstrate the *reasons why* people should buy from *your* business. And why it's the only obvious choice.

You've heard the saying *'out of sight, out of mind'.* Well, that's the real risk you run if you draw back on marketing when things get a little challenging out there. But guess what? Tougher times also present a huge opportunity for you to shake off what's holding you back, to releasing you to flourish and grow.

When everyone else is withdrawing and going quiet, the business that continues to connect, engage, and deliver exceptional value consistently, will be the ONLY one customers remember – and stay loyal to – way after any downturn becomes history.

Step by step, I take you through 21 ways to *guarantee* you retain your best customers; enhance your digital presence; and get creative with your marketing content, to kick-start rapid sustainable growth. You'll learn how to harness the immense power of email marketing; tell the story behind your business authentically to build trust and credibility; and even tap into *'hyper-local'* marketing to strengthen community ties with you and your business.

I explore and delve deep into all this in a way that is relatable, practical, and totally actionable. All I ask of you is that you put these highly effective methods and strategies *into action*. This is important. It does you no good whatsoever to just *learn* what to do. You have to *do* it to see and enjoy the results.

Taking action is the key to your future success.

One more thing, if you're looking for a marketing guide that's stuffed full of high-level fluff, pure academic theory, and totally unrealistic expectations, that also needs a truck loud of money to put into practice – this isn't it. Instead, ***21 Ways To Grow Your Business...*** is about showing you step-by-step how to meet your customers' desires, their wishes, wants and needs – with the resources you already have – and putting them to use

EFFECTIVELY. It's about strengthening your credibility, keeping your business visible, trustworthy and above all... *indispensable*.

So let's dive right in. Let's reimagine your business growth in ways *proven to work* relentlessly during tough times, and will continue to do so well into the future. Welcome to your master blueprint for business success, resilience, consistently strong growth, and lasting good fortune.

Just before we begin, I feel I should clarify something first. I do apologise if I'm 'teaching granny to suck eggs' here but it's just that I so often hear the terms *'customer'* and *'client'* used interchangeably. However, they do have distinctly different meanings reflecting the nature of the relationship between a business and the person, or entity, it serves.

So, if you'll indulge me for a minute...

CUSTOMER: A Transactional Relationship

A customer typically engages in a transactional relationship with a business. This means a customer purchases a product or service, often without a long-term commitment or ongoing interaction beyond the sale. The focus is on the exchange of goods or services for money.

Customers typically have:

> Short-term engagement: They buy once or very occasionally, with no deeper personalised relationship.

Less personalised service: The interaction tends to be standardised, focusing on the product or service itself.

Immediate needs: Customers usually make purchases to fulfil a direct and often immediate need.

Examples of a customer include someone buying groceries, clothes, or a single service such as a haircut. The interaction is focused on the transaction itself.

CLIENT: A Relationship-Based Approach

A client, on the other hand, tends to have a more personalised, ongoing relationship with a business or professional service provider. In many cases, the term 'client' is used in industries where the service provided is continuous or requires customised attention based on specific needs.

A client relationship is characterised by:

Long-term engagement: A client typically works with the product or service provider over a period of time, often in a more consultative role.

Personalised service: The provider tailors services to the client's individual requirements, offering advice, expertise, and/or ongoing support.

Consultative or professional interaction: Clients are often seen in sectors such as legal services, consulting, marketing, and healthcare - where a service provider advises or assists a client over time.

For example, a marketing agency will have clients they work with on multiple campaigns over time, providing strategic guidance and support.

Purely for the sake of simplicity, throughout this book I refer to both customers and clients as 'customers', irrespective of whether your business serves customers or clients, or both.

Okay, ready to get started?

First, I strongly suggest you make lots of notes as you read through these pages. Tests have proven that when we write things down, we absorb the information 2 to 3 times more effectively.

Secondly, take **immediate action** on each strategy I share with you here. It does absolutely no good whatsoever just *knowing* what to do, if you do nothing with that knowledge. How is that going to work for you? I'll tell you how... it won't. TAKE ACTION!

Let's get going...

CHAPTER 1

Nurture Your Core Customers

Your core customers – the ones who've stuck with you through thick and thin – are more than simply buyers. They are the heartbeat of your business, the loyal supporters who already know, like, and trust you implicitly. These customers are your most valuable asset, even more so in tough times.

They've already chosen you as their go-to supplier of products or services, and with a little extra care, they will come back to you again and again. So now is the time to show them just how much they mean to you and your business.

Why Your Core Customers Are So Valuable

In the hustle to attract new customers, it's easy to overlook the goldmine that's already within your grasp. Your existing customers aren't just numbers on a spreadsheet – they're people who've already seen the value in what you offer. They've invested their time, their money, and their trust in you. This makes them incredibly valuable to you, especially when the economy starts to wobble.

During uncertain times, people crave stability. Your core customers know what to expect from you – they've experienced your products, your services, your ethos. They're not just buying something from you, they're buying into a professional relationship. And relationships, as we know, thrive on attention and care.

How to Nurture Your Core Customers

So how exactly do you go about nurturing these vital relationships? It's all about staying connected, offering value, and making sure your customers feel seen, appreciated, and genuinely special.

Here's how I suggest you go about it:

> Stay Connected: The foundation of any good relationship is *communication*. Regularly reach out to your core customers through the channels they are most comfortable with – whether this is email, social media posts, direct messages, or even an old-fashioned phone call. Remember those?
>
> The key here is consistency. Don't just pop up when you're launching a new product, or running a sale, keep the conversation going even when there's no immediate 'ask' involved.
>
> Share updates, helpful hints and tips, send them a free gift out of the blue, or simply check in to see how they're

doing once in a while. Your aim here is to stay top-of-mind and remind them that you're there, not just as a supplier, but as a partner who's investing in their future success and prosperity. After all, as they prosper and grow, so do you.

Offer Something Special: One of the best ways to give special attention and care to your core customers is by making them *feel* like they're part of something exclusive – a member of your inner circle, for instance.

This could be through exclusive special offers, early access to new products, or sneak peeks at what's coming down the pipeline. You might also offer a loyalty discount only available to returning customers, or create a VIP programme where your most loyal customers get first dibs on new releases.

When you offer something that's not available to just anyone and everyone, you're saying, *'You really matter to us'*. That special feeling of being valued as a VIP will go a long way in strengthening your professional relationship.

Even something as simple as a personal 'thank you' note can have a huge impact. Think about it, how often do you get a thank you note from your optician, or car mechanic, or shoe shop? It's so often the small things in business – and life in general – that make the biggest difference.

It's all about going the extra mile to show your core customers that you really appreciate their business and their loyalty.

Make Them Feel Seen and Appreciated: Everyone likes to feel special. Your customers are no different.

Personalisation is the key here. Use what you know about them to finely tune the way you make contact and the incentives you offer. If a customer always buys a particular product or service, offer them a special customer-only discount on a similar related item.

If you know a customer prefers a certain communication style, reach out to them in this way. The more you can make your customers feel like you really 'get' them, the more connected they'll be with you and your business.

As mentioned earlier, don't ever underestimate the power of a simple, heartfelt *'thank you'*. A genuine expression of gratitude – whether in an email, a social media shout-out, or a handwritten note – will make a world of difference. It's about acknowledging the role they've played in your current success and making it clear you don't, and never will, take their custom and loyalty for granted.

Build a Community Around Your Brand: Another powerful way to nurture and care for your customers is by creating a sense of community. People like to be part of something bigger, especially in unsettling times.

Consider creating a 'space' where your customers can connect with you and with each other. This could be a private Facebook group, a customer-only forum on your website, or even regular virtual meetups where your customers can share their experiences and learn from each other. Zoom works well for this, and it's free!

By fostering a sense of community, you're not just building stronger relationships with your customers – you're also giving them a reason to stay engaged with you. When customers feel like they're part of a close-knit, like-minded community, they are more likely to stick around, share their experiences freely, and even become an advocate for your brand.

The Long-Term Benefits of Nurturing and Caring for Your Existing Customers

When you take the time to nurture and care for your customers, you're not just securing short-term sales, you're building long-term loyalty.

These customers are more likely to stick with you through thick and thin; recommend your products to others; and even forgive the occasional trip-up because they know you have – in the final analysis – their very best interests at heart.

Increased Lifetime Value: When your customers feel valued and appreciated, they are more likely to continue doing business with you over the long term.

This increases their lifetime value to you, i.e. the total revenue you can expect to earn from a customer over the course of your relationship with them. And in tough times, that steady, predictable revenue is a vital lifeline to your business.

Word-of-Mouth Marketing: Happy, loyal customers are one of your your best marketers. They are the ones who will sing your praises to their friends, family, and colleagues, bringing new customers to your door without you having to spend a penny on advertising. And because word-of-mouth recommendations come from a trusted source, they are incredibly powerful in influencing people's purchasing decisions.

Stronger Brand Reputation: When you *consistently* nurture your customers, you are building a reputation as a brand that genuinely cares. Your business will stand out as special above all others.

This kind of reputation is priceless, especially in an age where consumers have more choices than ever before. A solid reputation will help you stand out in a crowded market and attract even more loyal customers.

Summary

Nurturing and giving extra special care to your core customers isn't about sending out a few extra emails half-heartedly, or offering the occasional discount. It's all about building and maintaining a strong relationship, based on trust, appreciation, and mutual respect.

It's about recognising the *real value* of that core of customers who have already chosen you, and showing them that their loyalty is noticed, valued, special to you, and rewarded.

So, take the time to connect right *now*. Today. Offer something special. Make them feel seen and appreciated. Remember this: In the end, it's these special relationships that will carry your business through any stormy sea and will lay the foundations for your long-term success.

After all, in a world that's constantly changing, your existing customers are the ones you can count on. They should be able to count on you also.

CHAPTER 2

Deliver Exceptional Value

When people are watching every penny, your mission is crystal clear: you *must* make sure your potential customers see your products or services, not as an option, but as the smart, sensible and obvious choice. It's about showing people the options you offer are not merely 'worth it' – they are *totally indispensable* to them.

Why Delivering Real Value Matters More Than Ever

When budgets are tight, people become hyper-aware of how and where they're spending their money. They're not necessarily looking for the 'best deal' – they will be looking for the best overall *value*. There is a big difference!

Value isn't about the price; it's about what your customer receives in return for their money. It's about solving problems, meeting wants, satisfying needs and making their lives better in some meaningful way... easier, less stressful, more comfortable, less painful.

Especially in a tough economic environment, people aren't just buying products or services – they are buying *solutions*. They're buying peace of mind, convenience, comfort, happiness. In short... relief from a *'pain-point'*, whatever that might be in each individual case.

Your mission as a business owner, is to identify the pain-point, to make it abundantly clear how your offering delivers a lasting solution to their problem, and how they will be missing out if they don't choose your solution. Also make it crystal clear *why* and exactly *how* they will be missing out, leaving no doubt in their mind.

How to Deliver Real Tangible Value

So how do you go about positioning your solution as the only smart and sensible choice in your customers' eyes? Well, it's all about understanding their needs and wants; empathising with their situation, making your *value proposition* impossible to ignore.

Let's break it down:

Introduce Budget-Friendly Options: First things first – meet your customers where they are right now. By that I mean, if your typical offering tends to be out of reach for some during tough economic times, consider introducing budget-friendly options. This doesn't mean slashing prices across the board, it means finding creative ways to offer something that's both affordable and at the same time of high perceived value.

Maybe it's a simplified, 'lite' version of your product, or service, that still delivers core benefits. Or perhaps it's a special package deal that offers more value at a slightly lower price point. The key is to make sure these options still reflect the quality and reliability your business is known for, so your customers feel like they're getting a great deal without sacrificing quality.

Bundle Your Offerings: Another great way to deliver more value is by bundling your products or services. When you package complementary offerings together, you're not just selling individual items – you're providing a comprehensive solution.

For example, if you operate a gym, you could bundle workout classes with nutrition plans, or offer a year's worth of classes for the price of ten months. The idea is to give your customers more 'bang for their buck' while making it easier for them to achieve their personal goals.

Bundling is also a way to introduce customers to more of what you offer, which can lead to increased loyalty and higher lifetime value. They get more, you earn more. Everyone wins.

Focus on Problem Solving: At the heart of delivering real tangible value is the ability to solve your customers' problems. Take a step back and think about what your customers are actually buying from you. What pain-points are they looking to ease? What needs or wants are they trying to fulfil?

Once you have a clear understanding of this, you can easily tailor your message to highlight how your product or service directly addresses these issues.

For instance, if you sell organisational tools, emphasise how they save time, save money and reduce stress. If you are a financial consultant, focus on how your services help people save money, grow wealth, and navigate uncertain economic times with confidence.

By positioning your offering as a *solution* to a specific problem, you make it easier for customers to see and appreciate the value you bring to the table.

Emphasise Long-Term Benefits: During an economic downturn, people are often hesitant to spend money on things they don't see as immediately necessary. This is where emphasising the long-term benefits of your product or service comes into play. Show your customers how investing in what you offer now, can save them money, time, and effort down the road.

For example, if you sell high-quality home appliances, highlight their durability and energy efficiency, which lead to savings over time. If you're in the business of online education, emphasise how learning new skills now, can lead to better job opportunities or increased earning potential in the future. By framing your offering as a wise investment, you make it easier for customers to justify the expenditure.

Make Their Lives Easier, Happier, More Comfortable: Delivering value is about solving a problem and enhancing your customers' lives in a meaningful way. This could mean making their daily routine a little easier by relieving stress and adding a layer of comfort to their lives.

Think about how your product or service can improve your customers' quality of life, even in a small way. Maybe your app saves them time, your skincare product boosts their confidence, or your meal delivery service takes the stress out of dinner time. When you communicate these benefits and results, you're not just selling a product – you're selling a better, easier, and more enjoyable life.

Positioning Your Business as the Smart Choice

Once you've identified how your business delivers real value, the next step is to communicate it effectively. This is not about listing features or touting discounts – it's about crafting a narrative that resonates with your audience on an *emotional* level. People don't choose what they buy with *logic*, they choose with *emotion*.

Use Customer Testimonials: One of the most powerful ways to demonstrate value is through the voices of your satisfied customers. Share testimonials, case studies, and reviews that highlight how your product or service has made a difference in their lives. Real stories from real people are incredibly persuasive, helping potential customers see the tangible, real-life results of why to choose *your* product or service.

Show and Tell: Whenever possible, demonstrate and show the value of your offering *in action*. This can be through videos, before-and-after comparisons, or interactive tools that let customers see for themselves how you are able to solve their problems. The more concrete and visual your proof-points are, the more compelling your value proposition becomes.

Be Transparent and Honest: In tough times, people value honesty and transparency more than ever. Be upfront about your pricing; the *benefits* of your product or service; and what customers can realistically expect. When you are honest about what you offer and how it can help, you build trust. Trust is a key component of perceived value.

Keep Your Customer at the Centre: Finally, always keep your customers' well-being at the forefront of everything you do. Understand their needs; empathise with their challenges; and make sure every aspect of your offering is designed with their best interests at heart, *at all times*. When your customers feel like you truly understand and care about them, they're more likely to see your product or service as *essential*.

Summary

Delivering *real* value isn't only about offering a great product at a fair price – it's also about making your customers feel like choosing you is the *smartest* decision they can make. It's about meeting their needs, satisfying their wants, solving their problems, and improving their lives in meaningful ways.

By introducing budget-friendly options, bundling your offerings, and focusing on problem-solving and long-term benefits, you position your business as the clear, sensible choice in your customers' eyes.

When you do this with transparency, honesty, empathy, and a deep understanding of what your customers are really looking for, you are delivering value for money and creating lasting relationships that will see your business through even the roughest of seas.

CHAPTER 3

Get Creative With Content

When the going gets tough, people naturally become more cautious about how they spend their hard earned cash. They're looking for reassurance, for expertise, and for businesses they can trust.

This is where your marketing content comes in, be it blog posts, sales letters, emails, website copy – and similar – as a tool for visibility, and as the very foundation of the trust and credibility you build with your audience. Content isn't just something you 'put out there'; it's how you become recognised as the go-to resource to be relied upon, especially when people are being careful with their budgets.

Why Creative Content is Vitally Important

In an economic slowdown, consumers are more deliberate and discerning in their purchasing decisions. They are not necessarily looking for the cheapest option – but they ARE looking for the *smartest* one. They want to buy from businesses that understand their stresses, strains, and struggles and can offer real solutions. This is where the quality of your marketing content comes into play. When done right, marketing content demonstrates your expertise, shows empathy for your customers' day-to-day challenges, and keeps you at the forefront of their minds when they're ready to make a purchase.

But here's the thing: it's not just about creating any content. It's about creating the *right* content – the kind that speaks directly to the concerns of your audience right *now*. It's about being helpful, practical, and relevant. It's about showing up consistently, so your customers know they can count on you for the insights and advice they are searching for.

How to Get Creative with Your Content

You don't have to reinvent the wheel when getting creative with your content. Instead, find fresh ways to connect with your audience and meet them in their space.

Let's explore how you can do this:

> Address the Challenges Your Customers Are Facing: Start by putting yourself in your customers' shoes. What are they really struggling with right now? What's keeping them up at night? What do they worry about all the time? Once you've identified their pain-point, create content that directly addresses their problem and show how you can solve it.

For example, if you're a financial advisor, you might create content around budgeting tips during a recession, or how to protect investments during market volatility. If you run a small business consulting firm, you could share advice on how businesses can reinvent, adapt, or find new revenue streams in challenging times.

The goal here is to demonstrate to your audience you understand their situation and that you are here to help them navigate through it.

Choose the Right Formats: Content comes in all shapes and sizes The format you choose should align with how your audience prefers to consume information. Some might love reading in-depth blog posts, while others prefer watching quick informative videos, or scrolling through social media updates.

Don't be afraid to experiment with different formats to see what works best for your audience. If you are used to writing blog posts, try branching out into videos, or infographics. If your audience is active on social media, focus on creating bite-sized content that's easy to digest and share. The key is to meet your audience where they hang out and in the format they find most engaging.

Focus on Practical, Actionable Advice: When people are facing uncertainty, they are not just looking for information, they're looking for *guidance*. They want to know what they can do to improve their current situation. This is why your marketing content should always include practical, actionable advice that your audience can use immediately.

For instance, instead of just talking about the importance of customer retention, offer specific strategies your audience can use to keep their customers engaged. Instead of just highlighting the benefits of your product, show them exactly how it can help solve a problem they're facing. The more practical and actionable your advice, the more valuable your content becomes.

Be The Go-To Resource: Consistency is key when it comes to building trust and staying top-of-mind. You want your audience to think of your business as their go-to resource whenever they need advice, insights, or solutions. This means showing up regularly with content that's not only helpful but also timely and relevant.

Think about creating a content calendar that aligns with your customers' needs throughout the year. For example, you might plan content around key dates or seasonal challenges that your audience typically faces. You could also respond quickly to emerging trends or news stories that are relevant to your industry, positioning yourself as a thought-leader who's always 'in the know'.

Showcase Your Expertise and Empathy: Your content is also an opportunity to showcase your expertise and build trust and credibility. But remember, expertise isn't about showing how much you *know* - it's about showing how much you *care*. The distinction is important.

Use your content to demonstrate you understand the challenges your customers are facing, and that you're here to help. Share case studies, testimonials, and real-life examples of how you've helped others overcome similar challenges. Offer insights that are rooted in experience. Don't be afraid to let your personality shine through. People want to do business with people they feel a connection with. A warm, empathetic tone goes a long way in building such a connection. Remember, people buy from people, not faceless entities.

Creative Content Ideas to Get You Started

Need some inspiration? Here are a few ideas to help get you going:

How-To Guides: Create detailed 'how-to' guides that walk your audience through solving a specific problem. For example, if you're in the home improvements industry, you could create a step-by-step guide to small, budget-friendly DIY projects that can enhance a living space without breaking the bank.

Case Studies: Showcase customer success stories. Highlight how your product, or service, helped them achieve their goals. This builds trust and also provides social proof that your offerings deliver real results.

Interactive Content: Consider creating interactive content like on-line quizzes, calculators, or assessments that help your audience engage with your business in a fun and personalised way. For example, a financial planner could offer a 'Budgeting in a Recession' calculator, while a fitness coach might create a 'Find Your Perfect At-Home Workout' quiz.

Video Content: If you are not already doing so, now is a great time to get into video content. Whether it's quick tips; in-depth tutorials; or a behind-the-scenes peek into your business, video is a powerful way to connect with your audience. Plus, video content is highly shareable, which helps to expand your reach.

Webinars or Live Q&A Sessions: Host webinars or live Q&A sessions where you interact directly with your audience, answer their questions, and offer valuable insights. This not only positions you as an expert but also gives your audience a chance to connect with you in real time.

Summary

Getting creative with content is about more than just putting words on a page, or videos on a screen. It's about creating a genuine connection with your audience by understanding their problems, empathising with their challenges, and offering real, practical solutions. It's about being the go-to resource they can turn to, time and again, because they know they can trust you to always deliver great value.

When you focus on creating content that is relevant, actionable, and empathetic, you keep your business top-of-mind; you build lasting relationships that will carry your business through even the most challenging times.

So, roll up your sleeves, get creative, and start crafting marketing content that truly resonates with your audience. The trust and connection you build through your content will keep your business strong and build for the future to go on to great success.

CHAPTER 4

Strengthen Your Digital Presence

In times of uncertainty, the online world becomes a lifeline for connection, information, and decision-making. Whether your audience is looking for advice, shopping for essentials, or just seeking reassurance, they are searching the Internet to find it for certain. This is why your digital presence isn't just important – it's absolutely *vital*.

Digital presence goes deeper than just having a website, or a few social media accounts. It's about being present and engaging in the spaces where your audience spends their online time. It's about making sure your online platforms are not just functional, but inviting, informative, trustworthy, and easy to navigate.

In a world that's increasingly digital, your online presence is often the first – and sometimes the *only* – impression you make on your potential customers. So, make it a good one.

Why a Digital Presence is Vitally Important

People crave stability and certainty. They want to do business with people they can trust to deliver. Trust these days often begins online. If your digital presence is strong, it can be the cornerstone of your customer relationships, giving them confidence in your message, especially in unpredictable times.

On the flip side, a weak, out-dated, or non-existent digital presence can quickly erode that trust, raising questions in your potential customers' minds as to whether you really are the right choice for them.

Your website, social media accounts, and online ads are all *critical* touchpoints, where you can either draw people in, or lose them entirely. This is where you communicate your business's value, showcase your expertise, and build connections.

In many cases, this will be the *only* deciding factor on whether a potential customer chooses you or one of your competitors. So get it right.

How to Strengthen Your Digital Presence

So, how do you make sure your digital presence is not only solid but truly exceptional? Here's how to get started:

Optimise Your Website for Search Engines: First things first – if your website isn't search engine friendly, you're missing out on a huge opportunity. SEO (Search Engine Optimisation) is about making sure your website ranks highly in relevant searches, so people can find you when they need you most. Start by conducting keyword research to understand what terms your potential customers are searching for. Then, incorporate these keywords naturally into your website content, meta descriptions, and headings.

Don't stop there, thinking the job is done.

Beyond keywords, make sure your website is structured in a way that search engines can easily understand and find their way around. This includes having clear navigation, using descriptive URLs, and ensuring your website is also mobile-friendly. The easier it is for search engines to crawl and index your site, the better your chances are of appearing in those all-important search results.

Prioritise Speed and Mobile-Friendliness: In today's fast-paced world, people expect websites to load quickly and work seamlessly on any device. If your site takes too long to load (more than 2 or 3 seconds), or if it isn't easy to read on a smartphone, you could be losing customers before they even see what you have to offer.

Start by testing your website's speed using tools such as Google PageSpeed Insights or Pingdom. If your site is slow to load, consider optimising your images, using a content delivery network (CDN), and minimising unnecessary scripts or plugins.

Don't forget mobile users – make doubly sure your website is 'responsive', meaning it automatically adjusts to look great – and read well – on any screen, including tablets, pads, and phones. This isn't just a 'nice-to-have'; it's absolutely essential, since more than half of all web traffic comes from mobile devices these days.

Engage Actively on Social Media: Social media is where a vast swathe of your audience goes to connect, share, and discover. It's where they can learn about your products and/or services, ask questions, and experience how you interact with your customers and potential customers.

In other words, it's a *critical* part of your digital presence overall.

But simply having social media accounts isn't enough on its own – you must be active, engaged, and responsive. Start by identifying which platforms your audience uses most. Is it Instagram? LinkedIn? Facebook? X (formerly Twitter)?

Once you know where they are, focus your efforts there. Share content that's relevant, helpful, and aligned with your business persona. Engage with your followers by responding to comments, answering questions, and participating in conversations. The goal here is to create a vibrant, engaged community around your brand.

Create Content That Resonates: As previously discussed, content is the heart of your digital presence. It's what attracts people to your website, keeps them on your social media pages, and encourages them to engage with you. To strengthen your digital presence, focus on creating content that is in tune with your audience.

This can be blog posts, videos, infographics, or social media updates – whatever format best suits your message and your audience's preferences. The key is to make sure your content is valuable, useful, relevant, and in-tune with the interests of your audience.

Address their pain points, answer their questions, and provide insights to help them navigate the challenges they're facing. When your content is genuinely helpful, people will keep coming back for more – additionally they will be more likely to choose you when they're ready to make a purchase, because you have demonstrated your knowledge, expertise, credibility, and trustworthiness.

Use Targeted Ads to Reach Specific Audiences: In uncertain times more than ever, every pound (dollar or euro) you spend on marketing *must* return *at least* one pound and one penny in revenue. That's why it's vitally important to make sure your ads are reaching the right people, i.e. the ones who are most likely to need, or want, the particular solution you are offering right now.

This is where targeted ads come into play.

Platforms like Google Ads and Facebook Ads allow you to target *specific* demographics, interests and behaviours, so that you can reach the *exact* people who are most likely to respond to your message.

For example, if you're a supplier to the local population, you can target people in your immediate locality. If you offer a service particularly relevant to a certain age group or profession, you can target these specific markets. The more precise and laser-focussed your targeting is, the more effective and profitable your ads will become.

At the same time, don't forget retargetting – showing ads to people who have already visited your website, or engaged with your content. Retargeting is a powerful way to stay top-of-mind and encourage these potential customers to take the next step towards buying your product or service.

Monitoring and Adapting a Digital Strategy: Strengthening your digital presence isn't a one-off task – it's a continuing and ongoing process. The digital landscape is forever changing, and so are your customers' needs, wants, desires and behaviours. This is why it's extremely important to regularly monitor your digital performance and be ready to adapt your strategy as needed.

Use analytics tools to track key metrics such as website traffic, social media engagement, and ad performance. Look for trends and patterns that can help you understand what's working and – just as importantly – want isn't working. And don't be afraid to experiment with new tactics or platforms.

The more you learn about your audience and how they interact with your online marketing, the better you can tailor and tune your digital presence to meet their needs.

Summary

Your digital presence is the foundation of your brand in the online world. It's how you connect with your audience, build trust, and showcase the value of what you offer the marketplace. By optimising your website, engaging on social media, creating resonant content, and using targeted ads, you can ensure your digital presence is not just strong, but truly *exceptional*.

People search the Internet for answers, guidance, support, and solutions. By strengthening your digital presence, you position yourself, and your business, as the reliable, trustworthy choice that's there for them, no matter what.

Take the time to invest in all your online platforms, to make sure your digital presence reflects the best of what your products or services have to offer. Your customers will thank you for it. As a result, the ongoing wellbeing of your business will be assured.

CHAPTER 5

Diversify Your Revenue Streams

Relying on only one source of income is like trying to balance on one leg with one arm tied behind your back – eventually, you're going to get wobbly, lose your balance and fall over. When the economy slows, or business gets tough for any reason, only one source of income is somewhat precarious to say the least. This is why diversifying your revenue streams isn't just sensible – it's downright *essential*.

Here's the thing...

When you set up additional ways for people to buy from you, you are quite simply opening more doors to more revenue. You are also creating a safety net for the survival of your business. You're no longer dependent on only one offering or one type of customer. In fact one of *anything* in life is generally not a good idea. You need some form of backup to be on the safe side.

When you are generating revenue from multiple sources, if one source slows down, another can pick up the slack. Think of it like turning your business into a multi-legged stool – solid, balanced, steady, and ready to weather whatever stormy weather comes your way. And it will at some point in time. It's inevitable. Diversifying your revenue isn't complicated. In fact, it's often a case of expanding on what you're already doing well.

Let's now take a closer look at how you can diversify effectively and in a way that aligns perfectly with your business and your customers...

Diversifying Your Revenue Streams is Crucial

First off, let's talk about why diversifying is so important. In good times, having one solid revenue stream might feel like enough. However, when the economy stutters, consumer behaviour changes and confidence is adversely affected. Also, if the particular industry you're in hits a slow period, that single source of income can quickly dry up.

Suddenly, the business that once felt stable, now feels decidedly shaky. Diversifying your revenue helps smooth out these bumps.

It's also a way to maximise your value to your customers. You've already worked hard to build relationships with them, so why not offer them *more* ways to benefit from your expertise, your products, your services? Not every customer wants or needs the same thing from you, so offering a variety of options lets you meet them right where they are.

The exciting thing is, your new revenue streams may well open up doors you hadn't even considered before. You might even discover a new market, a new customer segment, or even a whole new direction for your business. This is the power of allowing yourself room to develop and grow.

How to Diversify Your Revenue Streams

So, how do you go about diversifying without overwhelming yourself or diluting the benefits of the solutions you bring to the table? Start by thinking about complementary products and services that will fit naturally with what you are already offering.

You don't need to reinvent the wheel – just look for additional ways to expand on what is already working for you. Set your imagination free.

Here are some ideas to get you started:

> Launch an Online Course or Workshop: Since your are the expert in your field, why not package your expertise and knowledge into an online course, workshop, or webinar? Whether it's a full-scale programme, or a series of smaller bite-sized sessions, education-based products are a fantastic way to diversify your income. They are scalable, meaning you can create the course once, then sell it many times over without any additional overhead. Best of all, you're still delivering value by teaching your customers something that benefits them.

For example, if you run a small marketing consultancy, you could offer a course on DIY social media strategies for small business owners. It would be a natural extension of what you already do, and it gives you a way to help those who might not be ready to invest in full-on one-to-one consulting services just yet.

Offer Downloadable Resources: Digital products – eBooks, templates, guides, cheat sheets and checklists – are another great way to diversify your revenue. These are relatively easy to create, especially if you're pulling from existing knowledge or content you have already created. And just like online courses, they are scalable and can be sold to multiple customers without any additional time or expenditure on your part.

Think about what your audience might need or find useful.

A graphic designer, could offer downloadable design templates. If you're a fitness coach, you could create a series of workout plans or meal preparation guides.

Digital products serve as a low-cost option for customers who aren't in a position to invest in your high-ticket services, but still want to glean the value from tapping into your knowledge and expertise.

Introduce a Subscription Service: Subscriptions are the ultimate form of repeat business. They offer a steady, predictable income stream and help create long-term relationships with your customers.

Subscription services take many forms and depend on what kind of business you are in.

If you sell physical products, you can introduce a subscription box where customers receive curated items delivered to their door every month. If your business in a service sector, it could be a membership that gives exclusive access to premium content, monthly coaching sessions, or ongoing support. For example, a fitness studio, could offer a subscription that gives members access to a library of virtual workouts and nutrition plans.

Subscription plans keep your customers engaged, building loyalty over time. Plus, you're receiving regular and reliable income.

Create a Club or Community: People are willing to pay for access to exclusive content and experiences, or membership to a like-minded community. When you've built a strong and engaged following, consider offering a paid membership where customers get access to special perks, such as behind-the-scenes content, VIP Q&A sessions, or exclusive discounts.

If you're a writer, you could create a membership platform where subscribers get early access to your new work, personalised feedback on their own writing, or exclusive content you don't share publicly. The key is to offer something of high value which is available *only* to your most loyal followers.

Bundle Services and/or Products: Bundling is a great way to increase the perceived value of your offerings, while giving customers a more comprehensive solution. If you offer multiple services, package them together at a discounted rate. If you sell products, create themed bundles to solve a particular problem or issue.

For example, a business coach, could bundle a series of coaching sessions with an online course or an eBook. Or if you run an online shop, you could offer seasonal product bundles (think 'Holiday Survival Kit' or 'Self-Care Essentials') that encourage customers to purchase more than one item at at a time.

Bundling creates a win-win situation – your customers feel they're getting more bang for their buck, and you boost your income per transaction.

Don't get overwhelmed. You don't need to roll out a massive new revenue stream overnight. Start small. Pick one idea that feels most aligned with your brand and your audience, then test it. Maybe you start by offering a simple downloadable 'How To' guide. Or maybe you roll out a small subscription service for your most engaged customers.

Once you've tested the waters, encourage feedback from your customers. What do they like? What could be improved? Use this feedback to refine and repeat, until you've got a well-oiled revenue-generating machine.

Summary

In short, diversifying your revenue streams protects your business from downturns and slowdowns. It also promotes growth and offers opportunities to expand your range of products and services. By offering complementary products or services, you not only create a more stable foundation for your business, you also deepen your relationship with your customers. You give them more ways to engage with you, more reasons to stick around, and more value to benefit from by doing business with you.

Take a look at what you're already doing well. Think about how you can expand on that. Diversifying can be one of the most rewarding things you do for your business – both financially and creatively.

And who knows? You might just discover a whole new way to drive your business to even greater heights.

CHAPTER 6

Encourage Word-of-Mouth Marketing

In a world brimming with digital noise, where flashy ads and endless promotions vie for attention, there's one thing that still cuts through the clutter like nothing else: a genuine recommendation from someone who rates you highly.

Word-of-mouth marketing is powerful. More than that, it's a *superpower.* The best part? It's rooted in something money just can't buy... TRUST.

When someone really loves what you do – when your product or service genuinely resonates with them – they become more than customers... they become your *advocates*. They talk about you to their friends, to their family and to their colleagues. They share your story, because it's become part of *their* story. These first-hand, personal recommendations are pure gold. They carry more weight, more credibility, and more influence than any ad campaign could ever hope to achieve.

How do you harness the power of word-of-mouth marketing in a way that feels authentic and natural? How do you turn your happy customers into raving fans who can't wait to tell others about you?

Let's take a look...

Why Word-of-Mouth Marketing Works So Well

First things first, let's talk about why word-of-mouth marketing is such a game-changer. At its core, it's all about trust. People trust recommendations from people they know, far more than they trust ads. It's that simple.

When a friend raves about a product they've used, or a service they've experienced, you listen. You're more likely to give it a try because you trust and respect their judgment. And in times of economic uncertainty, that trust becomes even more valuable. People are more cautious with their spending, so they lean heavily on the experiences and opinions of those they know and who's opinion they trust wholeheartedly.

Word-of-mouth marketing is inherently social. It's about creating a ripple effect where one happy customer turns into three, and these three turn into nine, and so on. It's the kind of organic growth that feels natural and sustainable because it's driven by real experiences, not just clever marketing.

How to Encourage Word-of-Mouth Marketing

Okay, so we know word-of-mouth is powerful. But how do you encourage it? Here are some ways proven to work...

Set Up a Referral Programme: A referral programme is a structured way to reward your customers for spreading the word about your business. It's an all round win-win. They get a little something extra for their effort, you get new customers who already have a positive impression of your business.

Here's the key... *keep it simple*. Your referral programme should be easy to understand and easy to share. Think about offering a discount, a free product, or some exclusive access, as a reward for every new customer they refer. Make it so compelling that your customers can't wait to tell their friends about you.

For example, let's say you run a boutique fitness studio. You could offer your existing clients a free class, or a discount on their next package for every new person they introduce. To make it even more enticing, offer the new customer a special deal as well. In this way, everyone is getting something of value.

Create Shareable Content: People like to share content they have enjoyed in some way - something that's useful, funny, inspiring, or just plain interesting. Make it easy for your customers to talk about you by creating content they can easily share with their friends, family and colleagues.

Think about things like blog posts, videos, infographics, or social media updates, that are directly in tune with the interests of your customers. Perhaps it's a 'How-To' guide that helps them get more from your product, or a behind-the-scenes video that gives them a peek into how you operate. Whatever it is, make sure it's something they will want to share with their friends.

Don't forget to add easy sharing buttons or links in your content to make it as simple as possible for them to spread the word.

Highlight Customer Success Stories: People love a story, especially when they can see themselves in them. Highlighting customer success stories not only serves as social proof but also gives your customers a chance to shine. And when you make your customers feel good about themselves and their achievements, they are more likely to share their experience with others.

Feature these stories on your website, in your email newsletters, and across your social media channels. You could even create a special 'Customer Spotlight' section where you showcase how your product or service made a difference in their lives. This not only builds credibility but also encourages customers to share their stories with all those they come into contact with.

Offer Exceptional and Outstanding Customer Service: Never underestimate the power of outstanding customer service. When you go above and beyond the call of duty to solve a problem, make someone's day, or deliver more than expected, people sit up and take notice. They also talk about it.

Create *'wow'* moments in your interactions with customers – you know, those little unexpected touches that makes someone's day, or makes them feel special. Maybe it's a handwritten 'thank-you' note, a surprise discount, or a follow-up call just to check in with them. These small gestures leave a lasting impression, and they're the kind of things people love to share about you.

Engage Your Community: Word-of-mouth marketing is also about building a sense of community. When your customers feel like they're part of something bigger, they are more likely to talk about it. Create opportunities for them to connect, not just with you, but with each other.

This can be through online forums, social media groups, or even in-person events (when possible). Encourage them to share experiences, ask questions, and support one another. When customers feel they are an important part of a like-minded community, they will naturally want to bring others into it.

Make It Easy to Share: One of the most effective ways to encourage word-of-mouth recommendations is to make it easy for your customers to share their positive experiences of you and your business. Do this by including share buttons on your website, in your emails, your newsletters, and on your product pages. Create a custom hashtag for your brand, or a specific campaign, that customers can use when they talk about you on social media.

You could also create referral cards or digital invitations that your customers can pass on to friends and family. The easier you make it for them, the more likely they are to do it.

Show Appreciation: Finally, don't forget to show appreciation for the customers who make the effort to spread the word. Whether it's a simple *'thank-you'* note, a shout-out on social media, or a surprise gift, let them know that you value their loyalty and their willingness to recommend you to others.

Recognising your advocates not only strengthens their connection with your business, but also encourages them to keep spreading the word. It sends a message to others that you genuinely care about your customers – something that's always well worth sharing.

Summary

Word-of-mouth marketing isn't only about getting people to talk about your business – it's also about creating genuine connections and delivering *real* value.

When your customers love what you do, they'll naturally want to share it with others. When you make it easy and rewarding for them to do so, you create a powerful ripple effect that brings in new business, builds trust, and strengthens your brand.

Think about how you can tap into the power of word-of-mouth marketing. Set up a referral programme that feels natural and holds value. Create digital content that people want to share. Deliver *exceptional* service that leaves a lasting impression. Above all, show your customers you appreciate their loyalty and their willingness to spread the word.

At the end of the day, it's not all about marketing – it's about building lasting relationships. And that's something people will *always* talk about.

CHAPTER 7

Focus on Cost-Effective Marketing

When budgets are tight, every £ ($ or €) you spend on promoting your business must work harder than ever. Now is the time to embrace marketing strategies that pack a punch, without breaking the bank.

Let's talk about focusing on marketing channels that offer a high return on investment (ROI) while still being super cost-effective. Because let's be honest – you want to get the most 'bang for your buck'. Don't you?

The good news is, you don't need a massive budget to make a massive impact. You just need to be a little bit smarter, a little more strategic, and put your energy into the places where your audience already hangs out.

Email Marketing: Your Budget-Friendly Superstar

These days, email marketing is the workhorse in the world of business. It's reliable, ultra low-cost, and incredibly effective. If you are not already using email to stay in touch with your customers NOW is the time to start.

Why?

Because email marketing offers one of the highest ROI. Studies consistently show that for every £ ($ or €) you spend on email marketing, you can expect an average return of **38 times** that. That's a lot of value for very little investment.

Don't think of email marketing as blasting out endless sales promotions one after the other (*yawn*). Think of email marketing as a relationship-building tool. It's a direct line of communication into your audience, meaning you are able to create personalised, thoughtful and valuable messages that make your customers feel special, cared-for and connected to your business.

Email marketing is your chance to deliver high value, share insights, and foster the relationships you have with your customers. Every one of the emails you send out, should deliver just 3 important things to your subscribers... value, value and value.

So how can you use email effectively? Start here:

> Segment Your Audience: Group the subscribers to your email list based on their preferences, interests, or purchase history, so that you can send specific, tailored and relevant content to each member of each group.

Provide Value: Share useful tips, exclusive discounts, behind-the-scenes events, or early access to new products. Make your subscribers feel like VIPs.

Be Consistent, But Not Annoying: Send emails on a regular basis – weekly, bi-weekly, or monthly – so that your name stays top-of-mind without overwhelming inboxes. Always be seen as a welcomed guest, never an annoying pest.

Create Eye-Catching Subject Lines: Remember, the subject line is the first impression you make. Make it interesting enough so that the recipient is compelled to open your email. You only get one chance to make a first impression.

With the right content and a thoughtful approach, email marketing is your secret weapon for staying connected to your audience, without emptying your bank account.

Social Media: Build Relationships Without Spending a Penny

When used effectively, social media is an amazing (and free) marketing tool for you. You don't need to pay for ads to create a strong social media presence. Often the most impactful content is organic. The key? Be authentic, engaging and helpful.

Social media engagement is more about building relationships rather than pure sales generation. It's a place where you can connect with your audience, share your business's persona, and build a following over time. It's less about shouting *'Buy from me!'* and more about conversation, discussion, and engagement.

Here are a few tips for maximising social media as a cost-effective marketing tool:

> Pick The Right Platforms: You don't have to be everywhere. Focus on the platforms where your audience already spends time. Are they on Instagram? Facebook? LinkedIn? Choose the platforms that make the most sense for your business.
>
> Post Consistently: Regular, consistent posting keeps your name top-of-mind. There's no need to post every day, but you should be active enough so that people don't forget about you.
>
> Engage With Your Audience: Social media isn't a one-way street. Respond to comments, answer questions, and get involved in conversations. Engagement promotes long-term loyalty.
>
> Share Valuable Content: Think of your social media presence as a resource for your followers. Share blog posts, helpful tips, supportive videos, and customer experiences. Add value, entertain, and inspire your audience.

Leverage User-Generated Content: If your customers are sharing photos, reviews, or experiences of your products, be sure to showcase them. It's free promotional content for you and a great way to build a solid reputation.

Social media is your playground for creativity and connection. When you approach it with authenticity, your efforts will translate into long-term customer retention without having to spend a small fortune.

Joint Ventures: Team Up with Other Small Businesses

There is great power in joint venture partnerships, especially when looking for cost-effective ways to expand your reach. A joint-venture arrangement is when two (or more) businesses team up to share customers and promote each other's products or services. It's a marketing win-win – you are both getting more exposure, and neither of you has to pay for it.

Here's why it works so well…

When you partner with a business who has products and/or services that complement yours (and are not in direct competition with you), you are introducing your offerings to a whole new audience. And because that introduction comes from a trusted source (the business you're partnering with), it carries much more weight than traditional 'cold' advertising.

How to make a joint venture work well for you:

Choose The Right Partners: Look for businesses that align with your values and target a similar audience. If you're a local bakery, for example, you might team up with a nearby coffee shop, or florist.

Collaborate On Content: Write guest blog posts for each other's websites, co-host a webinar, or create a social media campaign that highlights both of your businesses.

Share Email Lists: With permission, you can share access to your email lists (or feature each other in your newsletters) to help both of you reach a wider audience.

Host a Joint Event or Giveaway: Consider hosting a co-branded event, either online or in person. You could also run a giveaway where customers have to follow both businesses on social media, or sign up for both newsletters, to enter.

The beauty of a joint venture is that it's a highly cost-effective way to tap into a whole new customer base. Since both businesses are benefiting from such a relationship, it feels less like a marketing exercise and more like community-building.

Summary

In the final analysis, cost-effective marketing is nothing about cutting corners – it's about being *smart* with your resources and focusing on what has actually proven to work. Email marketing, social media, and joint ventures are all powerful tools that don't require a big budget to make a big impact.

The trick here is to lean into what feels authentic and natural for your business. Focus on building relationships, and *always* look for ways to provide *more value* to your audience. And remember, you don't have to be everywhere or do everything. A few smart, well-executed strategies will get you further than trying to be all things to all people at all times.

Even on a shoestring budget, you can still build a loyal community, increase your visibility, and keep your business growing strongly and consistently, all the while staying true to what differentiates you and your business from all the rest.

CHAPTER 8

Refine Your Unique Selling Proposition

In today's crowded market, where competition is fierce and customers are inundated with multiple choices, your Unique Selling Proposition (USP) is your ultimate differentiator; your differentiating point of difference. It's the compelling reason why someone should choose your business over others.

Your USP is the essence of what makes your business distinct, different, valuable, and memorable. When times are tough, refining and communicating your USP effectively can be the game-changer that keeps you in business.

What Exactly Is a USP?

Your USP is a clear, concise statement that articulates what makes your product, service, or business different and better than the competition. It's not simply a slogan or tag-line; it's the promise you make to your customers, along with the unique benefit they receive when they choose you.

Think of your USP as the definitive answer to the question: *'Why should I buy from you instead of someone else?'*

Why Is a Compelling USP the Key to Your Success?

When a person is faced with countless options available to them, they will often make a quick decision based solely on which marketing message resonates most with their needs, wants, desires, or pain points.

With this in mind, your USP must...

> Cut Through The Noise: Helping you to stand out in a sea of similar offerings, making it easier for people to remember you.
>
> Create a Strong Brand Identity: A well-defined USP establishes your brand's position and sets the tone for all your promotional and marketing messages.
>
> Build Trust and Loyalty: When your USP aligns perfectly with your customers' requirements, and *consistently* delivers on that promise, it fosters trust and encourages repeat business.

How to Refine Your USP

> Revisit Your Core Strengths and Offerings: Take a step back and evaluate what your business does exceptionally well. What are the strengths, special qualities, or features that genuinely set you apart from everyone else? This could be anything from exceptional customer service; superior product quality; innovative features; or

years of expertise in your field, i.e. your are the recognised expert.

For example, if you're a boutique bakery, your core strength could be the use of organic, locally sourced ingredients to create unbeatable, artisanal treats.

Understand Your Target Audience's Desires: A strong and compelling USP is always rooted in an in-depth understanding of your target market. What challenges or problems are they facing? What do they value most? Look at your existing customer base, conduct surveys, read reviews, or engage directly with your audience on social media to gain insights into what they truly want and appreciate.

If your target audience is busy professionals, they might value convenience, time-saving solutions, or products and/or services that simplify their lives. Your USP should address this head-on.

Analyse Your Competitors: To refine your USP, you must know what your competitors are offering. Identify their strengths and weaknesses, and look for gaps or areas where you can clearly differentiate yourself. This will help you position your business in a way that highlights what makes you better than the rest.

For instance, if your competitors are known for being quick but lack a personalised service, you could emphasise the tailored, one-on-one attention you provide.

Identify What Truly Makes You Different: This is where the magic happens. Combine your strengths with your customers' needs and compare them with what is already available in the market.

Ask yourself these three questions...

1. What solutions do we provide that no-one else does?

2. How do we solve a problem in a way which is different or better than others?

3. What experience do we offer that makes our customers' lives easier, less stressful, and more enjoyable?

Your uniqueness might lie in the exceptional experience you provide, the level of expertise you bring to the table, or the ethical and sustainable practices you stand for. Remember, it doesn't always have to be about having the lowest price or the most features – it's about the *value* you bring to the table, and why *exactly* are you better at delivering that value than your competitors?

Craft a Clear and Compelling Message: Your USP should be short, clear, and easily understood. It needs to *instantly* convey why you are the very best choice. Avoid industry jargon or overly complicated language. Instead, focus on crafting a message which resonates emotionally and logically with your target market.

For example, if you are a fitness coach specialising in helping busy parents stay active, your USP could say something like this: *'Helping busy parents reclaim their health in under 30 minutes a day, without sacrificing a minute of family time'.*

How to Embed Your USP In All of Your Marketing

Once you've refined your USP, it's crucial to weave it into every aspect of your marketing and promotional channels:

Website: Make sure your USP is front and centre on your homepage, about us page, and product/service pages. It should be one of the first things visitors see when they land on your website.

Social Media: Incorporate your USP into your profiles, bios, posts, and customer experiences. Use visuals, and testimonials to reinforce the value of your point of difference.

Advertising and Promotional Materials: Whether it's in digital ads, print materials, or email marketing campaigns, your USP should be consistently highlighted to ensure a cohesive message across all touchpoints.

Customer Service and Sales Interactions: Train your team to communicate your USP clearly and consistently during every customer interaction. It's essential your customers experience your value differentiator first-hand.

To help inspire you, here are a few examples of companies with a memorable and effective USP:

FedEx: *'When it absolutely, positively has to be there overnight.'* This emphasises speed and reliability, making it clear why FedEx are the best choice for urgent deliveries.

TOMS Shoes: *'One for One'.* TOMS built its brand around the idea that for every pair of shoes purchased, a pair is donated to someone in need. This USP is rooted in social impact, which resonates strongly with their target market.

M&Ms: *'Melts in your mouth, not in your hand'.* Focuses on a unique product benefit distinguishing M&Ms from other chocolate sweets.

Keep Evolving Your USP

Your USP isn't something that needs to be set in stone forever. As market trends change; customer preferences evolve; your business grows; it's essential to revisit and refine your USP regularly.

Be open to adapting and adjusting your message to stay relevant, fresh, and in-line with precisely what your target market is craving for.

Summary

Refining your Unique Selling Proposition (or Differentiating Point of Difference) is about clearly defining *what* makes you different; exactly *why* that difference matters to your target market; and *how* you can communicate your point of difference in a way that resonates well and compels action.

When done right, your USP becomes the backbone of your business identity, and the driving force behind your growth and success – especially in a crowded and competitive marketplace.

CHAPTER 9

Prioritise Customer Feedback

Your customers are a treasure trove of invaluable insights. They are your best source for understanding how to fine-tune your offerings, improve the purchasing experience for them, and ultimately strengthen your business.

Customer feedback isn't simply helpful to you, I say it's pretty much essential. However, it's not enough to go to all the trouble of harvesting feedback from your customers, then do nothing with it. You *must* act on what they are telling you. Even more importantly, you must let them know you've listened and done something about it.

Customer feedback isn't a simple box ticking exercise, to say you've done that – it's an important ongoing two-way interaction. It's a great opportunity for you to understand what's working for your customers and what isn't. And if something isn't working too well, *how* are your going to fix it, and *when*?

Let's dig deeper into why you should be prioritising customer feedback and also why it's critical to your business success.

We'll also have a look at how to approach the implementation of feedback in a way which is seen to be authentic, is actionable, and of mutual benefit.

Why Feedback Matters (especially NOW)

In any economic climate, customers need to feel their voices are being heard, listened to, and acted upon. In challenging times, the need for reassurance grows even stronger. When customers are being more careful with their money, they need the reassurance they are doing business with a company that genuinely cares about *them*, not only their wallets.

Asking for feedback signals to your customers that their opinions matter to you; that they are not just another number on a sales report, but part of a community you genuinely value and care about. It's a way to humanise your brand and to create deeper, more meaningful relationships.

The bottom line? Customer feedback helps you make smarter business decisions. Your customers are living, breathing examples of what is working for them and what is not working so well. Are they loving how a particular product is delivering the results they expected? Or how a service you offer has made their lives easier, more comfortable in some way? Or are they struggling with a clunky checkout process? Or unclear and confusing product descriptions?

You really need to hear about these things, and take the appropriate action.

Customers' insights will point you in the right direction to help you make adjustments and tweaks to improve their overall experience of dealing with your business.

How to Gather Customer Feedback

So how do you glean, gather and collate this goldmine of information without overwhelming yourself, or inconveniencing your customers. Try this...

Surveys: One of the simplest and most effective ways to gather feedback is through surveys. Keep them short and sweet. No-one wants to fill out a 20-question form when they are pressed for time. Focus on key areas where you genuinely want insightful feedback. For example: product usage, service experience, and further suggestions for improvement.

TOP TIP: Include open-ended questions allowing respondents to share thoughts in their own words. Start your questions with *How, What, Why* and *When.* This will uncover gems you might not have even thought about previously.

TOOLS: Use software like SurveyMonkey, Typeform, or Google Forms to easily create and distribute surveys online.

Social Media Monitoring: Social media is a hotbed of real-time feedback, whether customers are tagging you directly or talking about you and your business in their feeds. Be proactive – don't wait for people to come to you with problems or praise. Regularly monitor mentions, comments and reviews.

> TOP TIP: Ask for feedback directly in your posts. It can be something as simple as 'How well is the *<new feature>* on our *<new product>* working for you?" or 'What can we do to improve *<your experience>* with us today?'.

Direct Communication: Sometimes the best feedback comes from one-on-one conversations. If you have a small, loyal customer base, don't be afraid to pick up the phone, send a personal email, or set up a Zoom chat to hear their thoughts. This kind of direct conversation is incredibly insightful.

> TOP TIP: Don't be afraid to ask tough questions, *'What is the one main thing we can be doing better?'* or *'What specifically has been frustrating about your experience with us overall?'* Honest answers from your customers will spark some of your best improvements. Make sure you are fully prepared for honest, hard-hitting answers. And ACT on them.

How to Act on Customer Feedback

Now that you've gathered all this valuable feedback, what next? The worst thing you can do is nothing. If you're going to ask for feedback, you need to be prepared to TAKE ACTION.

This doesn't mean you have to implement *every* suggestion, but it does mean you *must* show your customers you are listening and that their valuable input is driving meaningful change.

Analyse The Data: Look for patterns and trends in the feedback. If multiple people are pointing out the same issue, or asking for the same tweak or adjustment, this is a sure sign the issue well worth addressing. Prioritise the areas that will have the most impact on the overall customer experience.

TOP TIP: Divide feedback into specific categories - product improvements; service-level tweaks and adjustments; content preferences; etc. This way you can easily identify trends and take the appropriate action.

Implement Changes: Once you've identified areas for improvement, it's time to make changes. Whether it's fixing a recurring issue, enhancing a product feature, or adjusting your communication style – show your customers that their feedback is shaping the way you do business going forward.

TOP TIP: Start small. You don't have to overhaul everything at once. Pick a few high-impact areas to address first, then build from there.

Close The Loop: Here's the bit far too many businesses forget to do – tell your customers what you've done with their feedback. Closing the feedback loop not only shows that you are responsive, but it also strengthens the bond with your customers. People like to know that their input is important and is driving change for the better.

TOP TIP: Share the changes you've made in an email, blog post, or social media update. Frame it as, *'You spoke, we listened'.* Show them how their voice is making a difference.

Publicly acknowledging your customers for their valuable feedback, makes them feel valued and also promotes a sense of community.

The Ripple Effect of Prioritising Feedback

The magic of prioritising customer feedback is in the creation of a virtuous cycle. When customers see you are listening and acting on their suggestions, they are more likely to provide feedback in the future. It deepens loyalty and encourages more honest and open communication.

In short, you're building a two-way relationship based on mutual respect. And that relationship? It's the cornerstone of long-term success and prosperity.

Summary

In today's climate, customer feedback is a lifeline. By actively seeking input from your customers; listening to their comments and concerns; and making improvements based on them, you're not only improving your business – you're also strengthening the relationship between it and the people who matter most to it.

So go ahead... ask, listen, act, rinse-and-repeat. You'll build trust, improve your offerings, and create a business that's more resilient in the face of any challenges that come its way, now and in the future.

CHAPTER 10

Create a Sense of Urgency

When the economy slows, people tend to hold onto their money a little more tightly. They'll carefully weigh up their options, take longer to make decisions and, sometimes, even talk themselves out of buying something entirely. Indecision is the enemy of action.

This is where 'urgency' plays a part. When done right (and ethically) creating a sense of urgency gives your customers a reason to act *now* instead of waiting until sometime later, or worse still... never.

Creating a sense of urgency is nothing about being pushy or aggressive. Nor should it be. That kind of unrefined approach only repels people. Urgency is all about gently nudging people to make the decision to buy now, and giving a genuine reason why they should act now, while reinforcing the value and benefits of your product or service.

Let's explore how to create urgency in a genuine way (important) that motivates immediate action, and ultimately helps your prospect to make the right decision that benefits them.

Why a Sense of Urgency Works

Human nature is interesting. We all have the best of intentions, but when there's no pressure to do anything decisive, we are the very best at putting things off. Whether it's signing up for a service, buying a product, or even clicking the 'add to cart' button – we all tend towards delaying decisions.

Why? Because we think we have all the time in the world. There's no immediate need, no pressing deadline, no fear of missing out. Then there's that niggling voice in your head... *'do I really need this today?'. 'Is it the right thing for me?'.*

This is precisely why creating an air of urgency works so well. It taps into the basic psychological trigger – FOMO – the fear of missing out on something good or particularly beneficial to our lives.

When you sense something is scarce – time-constrained, of limited availability, or exclusive – and you're like the rest of us, you will feel you should act sooner rather than later. After all, you don't want to miss out on a really good deal, or special offer, just because you left things too late. Do you?

Keep It Honest. Genuine and Authentic

Introducing urgency only works when it's real. Don't *ever* be tempted to make it up, or over use it. If you're constantly running *'limited-time'* offers or *'end-of-season'* sales that never seem to end, you'll get found out. People will switch off to your message. When this happens all credibility and trust flies out the window.

So, when you urge your audience to *act now,* make sure the reason is based on something real. Maybe it's a genuine limited supply, an actual deadline, or a special event that expires within a certain time and warrants acting right now. The more authentic, honest and transparent you are in the reasons *why* immediate action is needed, the more effective your message will be.

How to Create a Sense of Urgency- Ethically

Let's now get down to the practical side of things. Here are a few tried-and-tested ways to create an air of urgency that genuinely encourages and urges action, without making your reader, or listener, or viewer, feel like they are being manipulated, or coerced in some way.

> Limited-Time Offers: One of the most classic (and very effective) ways to create urgency is through limited-time offers. When your prospective customer know they only have a certain window of opportunity to take advantage of a discount, a special deal, or a time-limited promotion, it gives a clear reason to act *now.*
>
> The key here is making sure the window of opportunity is crystal clear – i.e. 24 hours only, a weekend sale, or a 5-day promotion.

Think about running a special promotion tied to a holiday, a new product launch, or even an end-of-season sale. Make it clear your offer won't last forever- and that action must be taken now to grab the deal, before it's gone for good.

> TOP TIP: You can make the offer even more compelling by adding a countdown timer on your website, or in your email, to visually reinforce the limited time available. BUT, and this is a BIG BUT... when the timer runs out DO NOT continue the offer, or reset the counter. You will be found out and people will turn away in their droves. Be honest, ethical and authentic at all times.

Limited Availability: When you have a product or service that is in high demand but of limited supply, the scarcity creates a powerful sense of urgency. We all tend to want what we can't have, or what might run out soon. So, if your product is only available in limited quantities, or for a short time, let your audience know – urgently.

Highlight when stock is running low, or if there are only a few slots left for a special offer or event. For example, *'Only 9 items left'* or *'Just 3 seats remaining on our upcoming workshop"*. In this way, the motivation to act quickly before the opportunity is missed is very high.

> TOP TIP: Make sure the scarcity is real. If you are constantly putting out 'limited availability' announcements, but always have plenty of stock, customers will eventually catch on and ignore you.

Exclusive Offers For VIPs: We all like to feel special. Offering an exclusive deal for a select group of customers – such as your email newsletter subscribers, loyal repeat customers, or social media private group members – creates exclusivity and a feeling of privilege. It's not just about *anyone* being offered the deal, it's strictly limited to a privileged few. Your inner circle, so to speak.

Let your VIP customers in on an exclusive early-bird discount, a members-only sale, or a private viewing on the launch of a new product. Be sure to emphasise that they are getting first dibs – before anyone else has a chance to buy.

> TOP TIP: Time-limit your exclusive offer to maximise the urgency factor. For example, *'As one of our most loyal customers, we're giving you exclusive 48-hour early access to our brand new collection, before going on general sale'.*

Seasonal or Event-Driven Urgency: Tie your urgency to a specific season, holiday, or event. This can feel more natural and aligned with your customers' lives, since it's linked to something they are already thinking about. Whether it's a back-to-school sale, a holiday promotion, or a special launch event, these moments create a built-in reason for your customers to act immediately.

Create seasonal promotions with clear start and end dates. You can even add urgency by incorporating special bonuses that are only available during this time.

> TOP TIP: Don't forget to remind your audience as the deadline approaches. Send a last-minute email or social media post to give a final nudge: *'Only 12 hours left to grab this deal'.*

Price Increases: Let your customers know if the price of your product or service is going up soon. This kind of urgency motivates people to buy now, while they can still lock in a lower price. It's also a great way to increase sales before a major launch or rebranding.

Clearly communicate when the price will increase and add a 'call to action'. For example, *'Our rates are increasing by 9% on 1st October – sign up now to lock in the current price'.*

> TOP TIP: Don't make price increases appear arbitrary. Explain the value behind the price change, whether it's because of new features, enhanced services, or increased demand.

The Gentle Nudge: Don't Overdo It

Promoting a sense of urgency is an undoubtedly powerful marketing tool. Having said that, be sure to use it sparingly and wisely. You don't want to be known as the business that always has a sale on that's *'ending tomorrow'* – we all know of at least one – or a product that's always *'almost sold out'*.

If you overdo things, customers will start to tune out to your 'offers' because they know there's always another one coming round the corner soon.

Instead, think of an urgency element to your message as a tool to use sparingly as a valid marketing strategy. Pick your moments – is it a special promotion, a new launch, or an important one-off event? And remember, it's not all about driving up your sales, equally – if not more importantly – it's about helping your customers to make a wise and informed buying decision that's of benefit to them.

Summary

Creating a sense of urgency isn't about rushing people into making a hasty decision, which might prove to be the wrong one for them - it's about helping people appreciate why *now* is the best time to take action. This may be the opportunity to take advantage of a limited-time offer; exclusive access; or an imminent price increase. The goal is to gently and ethically nudge your prospect towards making a decision that is, at all times, the right one for them.

When you master this strategy with integrity, authenticity and honesty, you will not only increase your sales, you will also build trust and promote long-time loyalty from your customers. People will enjoy doing business with you. A happy customer, is a good customer.

CHAPTER 11

Enhance Your Visuals

We all know the saying, *'a picture's worth a thousand words',* right? Well, in small business marketing, it's arguably worth a lot more than that. Especially when the economy gets sluggish with everyone and their dog vying for attention, a strong visual message is what will make you stand out from the crowd.

It's the first impression you make; your silent storyteller; and – to be blunt – it can often be the deciding factor between a prospective customer choosing your business or defecting to a competitor.

During a downturn, enhancing your visual image is a strategic move which will reinvigorate the efforts you put into your marketing activities.

Why?

Because visuals speak directly to your audience's emotions. In times of uncertainty, we all need to feel connected, reassured, and confident in the choices we make. Strong, consistent visuals communicate all this without muttering a word.

So, let's talk about how to refresh your visual branding in a way that is aligned with who you are and how it connects deeply with your audience.

What Exactly Is Visual Branding?

Visual branding is more than a pretty logo. It's the entire visual identity of your business... the colours, fonts, imagery, and overall aesthetics that say, *'this is who we are'.*

It's the way you present yourself visually across all touchpoints, from your website, to your social media profiles, to the packaging your products come in.

Think of it as your brand's personality in picture form. If your business was a person, how would it look and feel? How would it *'dress'* online? During difficult times, when we are looking for stability, trust, and solid connections, your visuals can help create a perception of stability and confidence. And don't forget, in the eyes of your audience, perception is reality.

Why Refreshing Your Visual Branding Matters

When the economy gets bumpy, businesses often draw back and cut costs. While it's important to be mindful of your budget, there's one area where a little investment can go a long way: your branding.

Refreshing your visuals during a downturn will breathe new life into your marketing messages and promotional materials and also signal to your audience that you're still around, still here, still vibrant, and continue to offer fantastic value for money. Also a fresh look can make your brand feel relevant again. It shows you are adapting to the conditions, evolving with the times, staying well ahead of the curve. Do you think this will resonate well with your audience? You bet it will!

How to Enhance Your Visual Branding (without losing your identity)

You don't need a total rebrand to make an impact. Sometimes it's just about fine-tuning, tweaking and refining what you already have.

Here's a few ideas on how you can enhance your visual branding in a way that stays true to your business, while giving it that extra *'wow'* factor:

> Update Your Logo (keeping it recognisable): Your logo is the face of your business, and sometimes even the best faces need a little refreshment. Remember though – you are known and recognised by your logo, so don't stray too far from the original concept. Instead, think of small tweaks to modernise it. Maybe it's a change of font to something a little more modern, or a simplification of the design, or freshening up the colour palette.
>
> If your logo looks and feels outdated or overly complicated, then simplify it. Logos that are clean and easily recognisable are more memorable and also look

great across all digital platforms and print formats. Keep what is unique and true to your brand, and also find ways to make it more 'in vogue'.

> TOP TIP: Don't be afraid to test it out with your audience. Share your updated logo on social media and ask for feedback. Make your customers part of the process. They'll love that.

Refine Your Colour Palette: Colours have a direct impact on how your brand is perceived. Are your colours conveying the right message? We tend to gravitate toward brands that feel established, trustworthy, calming, and positive. Consider modifying your colour palette to better align with the emotions you want to evoke in your audience.

Use two (no more than three) main brand colours and stick to them consistently across all platforms – website, social media, emails, stationery, and packaging. You can freshen things up by adding an accent colour sparingly, or slightly adjusting the shades to feel more modern or on-trend.

> TOP TIP: Blue and green are often associated with stability and reliability, while warmer colours like orange and yellow evoke optimism and energy. Think about the emotional tone you want to set.

Invest in High-Quality Images: In today's visual world, quality matters. Grainy, low-resolution images make even the very best products look unappealing. On the flip side, high-quality, beautiful photos or videos will elevate your brand instantly. Whether you're selling physical products or services, invest well in visuals that showcase your offerings in the best possible light.

Hire a professional photographer or videographer, or invest in good quality equipment yourself. Capture not just the products, but the experience of using them. Show your customers what it looks like to engage with your brand – whether it's someone using your product, attending your webinar, or receiving your service.

> TOP TIP: Authentic, behind-the-scenes images also work wonders. They help humanise your brand and show the real people behind it. Mix these in with polished product shots for a more balanced and relatable visual identity.

Design Consistency Across All Platforms: Consistency is key when it comes to branding. Your visuals should look consistent and cohesive across all platforms – your Instagram feed, your website, your email newsletters, your blog. Consistency promotes recognition.

Make sure your fonts, colours, logo, and design elements are used consistently everywhere. If you're introducing new elements – like updated fonts or a new graphic style – be sure they are carried through from your social media posts, to your website banners, to your blog and even your printed materials.

> TOP TIP: Consider creating a simple brand style guide to keep things consistent, especially if you're working with freelancers. It'll ensure everyone is on the same page when it comes to your identity.

Use Video to Convey Your Message: If you haven't yet embraced video, now is the time. Video content is one of the most powerful tools you have to convey your message. It can be incredibly engaging when done right. It allows you to showcase your offerings in a dynamic, visually compelling way that text or still images just can't match.

Create videos that show your products in action, highlight customer testimonials, or even produce a behind-the-scenes look at your business operations. Keep the videos short, authentic, and focused on your audience's needs, desires, and challenges.

> TOP TIP: You don't need a big budget or fancy and expensive equipment to start with video. Even simple, well-lit smartphone videos can be

incredibly effective, as long as they're aligned with your brand and provide value to your audience.

Why Perception Is Reality (in your customers' eyes)

How you are perceived is how you are remembered. Your visuals aren't just about looking good – they are about shaping how your customers feel about you and your business. When someone lands on your website, or scrolls through your Facebook feed, those first few seconds of visual exposure will form their perception of you.

Do your visuals communicate trust, professionalism, and value? Or do they feel dated, inconsistent, or unclear? In your customers' world, perception is everything. Strong, consistent visuals help ensure that what they see matches the quality of what you offer.

Summary

Enhancing your visual branding is all about aligning your visual identity with your brand's values, message, and mission. It's about making sure your audience sees what you stand for the second they come across your business.

Whether it's updating your logo, refining your colour palette, or investing in high-quality images, these small changes will have a big impact – especially in a crowded and ever-more competitive market. In tough economic times, giving your visual branding a refresh shows your audience you are confident, moving with the times, evolving, and here to stay.

CHAPTER 12

Offer Flexible Payment Options

When money is tight, your products or services may begin to feel out of reach to your customers. They may want to buy from you – really and truly want to – BUT their budget is tight, and they just can't swing the full price upfront.

This is when flexible payment options come in to their own. Offering a variety of payment choices can turn a *'sorry, not right now'* into a *'yes please',* even when times are a bit difficult.

Why Flexible Payment Options Work

In an uncertain world, people get cautious when spending their hard earned cash. They often rethink purchases they might have otherwise made without a second thought when times were better. However, just because someone can't pay for something all at once, doesn't mean they don't want or need it, they may well be willing to invest in it over a period of time.

Flexible payment options are such a game-changer because they lower the immediate barrier of entry for your customers. By spreading out the cost, you are not only making your product or service more accessible – you are also showing you care and empathise. You're saying, *'I get it. Times are tough. Let's find a way to make this work for you.'* And that, right there, demonstrates you care and completely understand the situation your customer finds themselves in.

How Offering Payment Options Can Boost Sales

Think of it like this: the more ways you offer people to pay, the easier you make it for them to buy from you, and so increase your sales. Some customers can pay in full right away... great! But for those who can't, offering them easier payment methods can mean the difference between making a sale and losing one.

Put another way... when you offer payment options, you're making it easier for people to say *'yes, I'm buying now'.*

Options can be a buy-now-pay-later plan, an instalment plan, or a subscription service. Payment flexibility shows you are thinking about your customers needs before your own. When customers see you on their side and fighting for their corner, they are much more likely to buy from you – and also keep coming back.

Okay, let's break down some practical ways to make payment options part of your business model...

What Payment Options Should You Consider?

Instalment Plans: This is one of the most common and straightforward ways to offer flexibility of payment. Instead of paying for the entire product or service upfront, your customers can break the total cost into smaller, more manageable chunks, over a set period of time – think monthly, bi-weekly, or weekly instalments.

By spreading the cost over time, your product feels more affordable. It helps reduce *'sticker shock'* for higher-priced items, making it more likely the purchase will go through.

You can set up payment by instalments through a variety of online payment processors, most of which are easy to integrate into your website. Popular services like PayPal, Stripe, and Square offer instalment options which are quick and straightforward to set up.

Buy-Now-Pay-Later (BNPL): The 'Buy-Now-Pay-Later' model has exploded in popularity over recent years. For good reason. BNPL customers receive your product immediately and defer payment, either settling in full at a later date, or making smaller part-payments over time. This is especially appealing for higher-priced purchases where the full amount is not immediately available on hand for whatever reason.

Buy-Now-Pay-Later helps lower the immediate financial hit while still giving customers the satisfaction of getting what they want right now. It's almost like having your cake and eating it (who doesn't want that?). It's also particularly helpful in an economy where cash is tight.

Many BNPL services are available to businesses, including Afterpay, Klarna, and Affirm. These services handle the payment process, so that you get paid upfront, and they collect from the customer over a set time period. It's a win-win for all.

The Subscription Model: Offering a subscription, or membership, option is another smart way to offer payment flexibility, especially if your business involves recurring services or consumable products. Instead of asking for a one-off payment of the full price up-front, break it down into a monthly (or quarterly) subscription fee. This keeps customers engaged with your business for the long-term, plus the lower monthly cost makes it easier for your customer to justify the expense.

Subscriptions turn one-time buyers into recurring customers. Plus, it provides your business with a predictable income stream. Paying a smaller amount regularly, rather than a large sum up-front, is extremely attractive when cash flow is tight. Also make it easy for your customer to adjust their repayment amounts, or even cancel their subscription all together if they want to.

If you supply a product which is consumed over time – skincare products, coffee, or pet food for instance – the subscription model is a natural fit. If you provide a service, consider offering it as a club membership with exclusive perks, special discounts, and early-bird discount deals given only to subscribing members.

Discounts for Early Payments or Bulk Purchases: While you should offer flexible payment as an option, some customers will pay in full, IF you give an attractive incentive for doing so.

Consider a discount for buyers who choose to pay the full amount upfront, and for those who buy in bulk. This is a great way to reward your immediate buyers, while still providing payment options for others.

We all love a good deal, especially when we feel like we're getting more for less. Offering a discount for paying immediately, or for buying in larger quantities, encourages customers to commit right away.

This can be as simple as offering a 5-10% discount for full payment, or creating bundled deals where customers save money when they buy more.

Why Flexibility Isn't ONLY for Your Customers

Flexibility isn't all about making your customers happy, though this is vitally important of course. It's also a sensible move for the long-term health and well-being of your business.

Offering flexible payments has the potential to...

Increase Conversion Rates: When people feel they can manage the cost a lot easier, they are more likely to complete the purchase.

Boost Customer Retention: Flexibility builds trust and makes customers feel cared-for, which has the potential to lead to longer, loyal relationships.

Expand Your Customer Base: There will be some who may have ruled you out because they thought your product or service was way beyond their budget. Offering a range of payment options opens the door for reconsideration on their part, most likely leading to a sale.

Improve Cash Flow: Even though customers are paying over a period of time, payment systems like BNPL ensure YOU are paid upfront. This sees a more reliable revenue stream for you, especially during slower times.

Communicate Your Flexibility Clearly

Don't let your flexible payment plans go unnoticed. It's crucial to communicate the options available clearly and concisely on your website, social media accounts, email campaigns, and most certainly at checkout. Let your customers know you want to make it easier for them to do business with you.

Make sure the ways to pay are seen as soon as a browser starts to consider a purchase. This can be a banner at the top of your website, a note in your product descriptions, or a pop-up at checkout. Make absolutely sure the options for flexible payments are seen as available at all times.

Summary

Being flexible in the way customers can pay you, is more than a convenience for them, it also acts as a powerful competitive advantage for your business. In a world where financial uncertainty has the ability to stop potential customers dead in their tracks, your flexible approach to payments may just be the thing that nudges them from *'no thanks'* to *'yes please'*.

Whether you're offering instalment plans, Buy-Now-Pay-Later options, or a subscription service, you are removing barriers and making your products or services accessible to a far broader audience. Plus, you're showing your customers you care and are empathetic to their situation... you are here to help, not just sell. This is something they will never forget.

CHAPTER 13

Focus on Retargeting

We've all been there... you're quietly browsing online, minding your own business. You click on a product or service that's caught your eye. You're reasonably interested, but for one reason or another – maybe the phone rang, or you decided to *'think about it'* – you don't take your interest any further at that point in time.

A few days later (sometimes only a matter of a few hours or even minutes later) an ad pops up for that very same product, or service, your were looking at. It's essentially a reminder... *'oh yes, I was interested in that'.* So you return to the site, primed and ready to click *'Buy Now'.*

This very effective marketing tool is known as *retargeting*.

Retargeting Works (and why you should embrace it)

In a busy world full of distractions, people often need more than one reminder, or nudge, to make a purchase. This is especially true during an economic downturn when customers are more cautious about how and where they spend their money.

The very first time someone visits your website, or social media feed, the odds are they are in a *'researching'* frame of mind. The second or third time however, after seeing your product or service pop up again and again, they start to build a familiarity, a bond.

Retargeting helps you give that gentle nudge, that subtle reminder keeping your business top-of-mind for those who are interested, but not quite ready to buy, and need a little more time.

Think of it as a friendly reminder, not a cynical, pushy sales tactic. It's about re-engaging people who've already shown an interest but might need a few more touchpoints before they are really ready to commit. In today's world, where attention is fleeting and competition is fierce, retargeting is one of the most effective ways to turn people at the *'maybe'* stage into *'yes please'* buyers.

How Retargeting Ads Work

Retargeting allows you to show ads specifically to remind those who have already visited your website, checked out your product pages, or engaged with your social media content. These people are already in your orbit. They have shown an interested – they've browsed your shop, read your blog, or liked your Facebook post – but for whatever reason, they haven't yet converted to a buyer.

The key here is personalisation. With retargeting ads, you are able to remind people of what they were looking at, offer them an incentive to come back, or simply keep your brand front and centre while they make up their mind. It's like saying, *'Hey, remember us? You liked what you saw before. Come on back and let's make it happen.'*

Why Timing Is Everything: The Power of Multiple Touchpoints

The majority of people don't buy on the first visit. In fact, studies show customers often need five to seven touch points before they feel ready to make a purchase. Retargeting helps ensure your brand shows up for them multiple times during their decision-making process, by creating a sense of familiarity. The truth of the matter is, most people are more likely to buy from a business they recognise as familiar, credible and trustworthy.

When someone sees your ad pop up while scrolling through Facebook, Instagram, or Google after visiting your website, it doesn't feel random – it feels *relevant*. It gives them a reason to pause, rethink, and hopefully finish what they started.

Practical Ways to Use Retargeting

Website Visitors: Let's say someone visits your website, browses a few pages, maybe even adds something to their cart – then life gets in the way. What happens then? They leave without buying.

With retargeting, you can show ads to those temporarily lost visitors across several platforms – notably Google, Facebook and Instagram, reminding them of what they have left behind.

Set up retargeting campaigns using Facebook Pixel or Google Ads. These tools track visitors to your website and allow you to show ads specifically targeted at them, as they browse the web or their social media feeds.

Sometimes people just need a gentle reminder to come back. Maybe they were on the fence, or maybe they just got distracted. Your ad reminds them why they were interested in the first place.

Cart Abandonment: If you run an online store, you're probably all too familiar with the frustration of cart abandonment. Someone gets as far as putting an item in their cart and then, for some reason, they leave. This is where retargeting is a game-changer.

Set up dynamic retargeting ads to show the specific products left in their cart. You can sweeten the deal by offering a limited-time discount or free shipping to incentivise them to come back and complete the purchase.

These ads are tailored to exactly what the customer was interested in, so they feel highly relevant and personalised to them in particular. That little extra nudge (perhaps an inviting discount) can often be enough to nudge them into buying.

Engagement on Social Media: Retargeting isn't just for your website visitors. You can also target people who have engaged with you on social media – those who have liked, commented, shared, or clicked on one of your posts or ads. This is a great way to reconnect with people who are clearly interested but haven't yet made a purchase.

Use Facebook's Custom Audiences feature to retarget people who've interacted with your page, posts, or ads. These are people who are already paying attention, so your ad will feel like a natural continuation of their engagement with you.

Social media is where people hang out, so meeting them where they're at, with an ad tailored to their previous interaction, increases the chance that they will take the next step.

Email Retargeting: Email is another powerful tool in your retargeting arsenal. If you have an email list of people who haven't bought from you yet, or who haven't purchased in a while, a targeted email campaign will remind them of what they are missing.

Send a personalised email to subscribers who haven't yet converted, or those who've been inactive for a while. Highlight a special offer, showcase a new product, or simply remind them why they subscribed in the first place.

An email message is personal, and when you target it specifically to those who have already expressed an interest, it will come over as even more relevant. Plus, email is a highly cost-effective way to engage your audience on a platform they check regularly.

Crafting the Perfect Retargeting Ad

The beauty of retargeting ads is they allow you to be specific. Instead of a generic ad that tries to appeal to everyone, you can create ads that speak directly to where someone is in their journey with your product or service offering.

Here's how to make your retargeting ads highly effective:

Personalise the Message: Remind visitors of the specific product they looked at and the benefits of buying, or the service they inquired about and its particular way of solving their problem. Include images and further details of the product to jog their memory.

Add an Incentive: Give a *reason* to act *now...* a discretionary discount, a freebie, or a limited-time offer. Adding a small incentive can be the tipping point leading to a purchase.

Use a Sense of Urgency (sparingly): While creating a sense urgency is effective, do use it thoughtfully and in moderation. Countdown timers, *'last chance'* deals, or reminders of limited stock often encourages people to act quickly. Don't overdo it though, or it can be seen as pressure selling. And we all know that doesn't work.

Summary: The Long-Term Value of Retargeting

Don't look at retargeting purely as a means of closing a deal. Consider it more about nurturing relationships with your audience over time. The more they see your name, the more familiar, credible and trustworthy you will become. In tough economic times, trust s worth its weight in gold.

By showing up consistently and offering *value* at every juncture, you're not merely chasing the next sale – you are building a long-term relationship with your customers. Retargeting keeps you visible, relevant and top-of-mind. So when your audience is next ready to buy, you are the first name they think of.

CHAPTER 14

Turbo-Boost Your Email Marketing

Email marketing is the quiet hero in your marketing toolkit. It's not flashy, it's not loud like TikTok or Instagram, but gets the job done – and done very well. Email marketing shines through as a cost-effective (often free), personal, laser-focused marketing strategy.

The REAL magic of email marketing is it acts as a direct line to your audience. It lands directly into their inbox – a place they visit daily, if not hourly. t gives you the chance to speak directly to your subscribers without fighting for attention in somewhere like a crowded social media feed. And, let's face it, in times when people are cautious about spending money, this is exactly where you need to be – ready with helpful *useful* content, offers, top tips, handy hints, special reports and other free stuff delivering the *right* message at the *right* time, in the *right* place.

Let's take a look at how you can make sure your emails get through, get opened *and* get acted upon...

Segment, Segment, Segment

Yes I know, it's tempting to send out a *'one-size-fits-all'* email to your entire list of subscribers, because it's easy. However, this blanket, scatter-gun approach is the quickest way to lose subscribers.

Why?

Because not everyone on your list is in the same stage of their journey with you. Also, not everyone on your list has the same interests, or the same reason to subscribe to your emails.

Some are long-term customers, while others are only prospective customers or people who have shown some form of interest in what you have to offer, but haven't actually made a purchase yet. Each of these groups of people should be receiving something slightly different from you; something that will hold their interest.

Segmentation is your secret weapon here. It allows you to divide your email list into smaller, targeted, groups based on things like purchase history, engagement level, or demographics. This way, you can send personalised and relevant messages that resonate well within each group.

Start with basic segmenting, for example:

New Subscribers: People who have just joined your list. They need a warm welcome and an introduction to who you are, what you offer and why it is different and better that anything else out there, and how you can help.

Repeat Customers: These are your loyal supporters. They will appreciate sneak peeks, loyalty rewards, or the occasional heartfelt *'thank you'* for sticking around.

Lapsed Customers: People who haven't purchased in a while. Send them a *'we miss you'* message, maybe with a special offer to encourage them back to the fold.

Engaged Non-Buyers: Those who click through and open your emails, but haven't bought yet. Yes, they are interested, but perhaps they need a little more convincing.

Segmentation helps you avoid sending irrelevant content to the wrong people (no one likes that). Instead, you get to talk to each group in a way which feels personal, tuned and tailored to their specific interests.

When your audience can see that your emails are written *just for them*, they are more likely to take whatever action you are gently guiding them towards.

Personalisation

Using someone's first name in your email message is a friendly touch. However, true personalisation goes way beyond that.

Personalising your emails is about making your audience feel like you get them; you fully understand their challenges; their needs in life; their wants; their desires; their pain-points and the solutions they are searching for.

For example, when a customer buys a product from you, follow this up with a *'how's it going?'* themed email. Show you are genuinely interested. Suggest additional uses for the product they have bought. Ask for feedback, good or bad, and perhaps also suggest complementary products which will further enhance their experience of your solution to their problem.

Similarly, if someone has been browsing through a particular category on your website, send them an email with recommendations from that category, or an exclusive offer that will go towards resolving their issue, or problem, or for any other reason they're searching through your website.

QUESTION: What makes email personalisation really come into its own?

ANSWER: Timing.

Yes, *timing* is very important. Send your emails at the *right time.* In other words, precisely when your customers are most likely to read them and take action. Maybe it's sending a follow-up a few days after they've browsed your website, or a friendly reminder when they've left items in their shopping cart. Tools like automated email sequences can help you do this seamlessly and effortlessly.

Okay, so now that we are sending the *right* emails to the *right* people at the *right* time... now what?

Deliver Exceptional VALUE- Every Single Time

The delivery of exceptional value, every time, lies deep within the heart of every successful email marketing campaign. Without doubt.

If your emails are focused only on making a sale, you will fail spectacularly. You will very quickly lose your subscribers. The number of unsubscribe requests will go through the roof. No-one on this planet will *ever* tolerate being 'sold to'.

Conversely, when your emails contain ONLY helpful, useful, valuable, usable information, such as hints, tips, insights, advice, or free stuff – you will not only *keep* your subscribers, they will eagerly await your next message, open it, and read it as soon as it arrives. Because they know it will be of use and benefit to them in some way.

How To Deliver Value in an Email

Think about what your subscribers care about most. Are they looking for hints and tips... special discounts... behind-the-scenes insights... help and advice... guidance?

When you turn up in their inbox with something that *genuinely* helps, you're not an annoying pest trying to sell them something, you are a welcome guest; you are a partner with a solution to their problem; you are making their life better, more comfortable, less stressful, more fun.

Here are a few ideas of how to pack exceptional value into your emails:

> Share Useful Content: Write *'how-to'* guides that help your audience solve a problem they are facing. Attach them to your emails. Make it clear *why* it's worth their time to read them.
>
> Exclusive Offers: Give your email subscribers a little something extra. Whether it's a special discount; early access to a sale; or a free resource of high perceived value. Make it so they 'get' why being on your list is a really good idea and of great value to them which comes with loads of benefits and special deals.
>
> Check-In and Ask for Feedback: Sometimes, giving value isn't all about offering something tangible. A simple *'how are you doing?'* or *'how can we help?'* email

can go a long way in building a strong relationship. It shows that rather than being hell-bent on selling something, you are more interested in listening to worries and concerns and helping them to find an answer.

Keep It Consistent and Relevant

Consistency is key with email marketing. It's really not enough to pop into your subscribers' inbox randomly, every once in a while with some irrelevant, off the wall ramblings. You should, at all times, present a reliable, consistent and professional persona. This can be in the form of a weekly newsletter, monthly updates, or a sequence of follow-ups after a purchase.

Consistency builds trust and also keeps you and your business at the forefront of your subscribers' minds. You will be the very first on their list when they need help with a solution to a problem they know you will have the answer to.

Why?

Because you have demonstrated you know what you're talking about. Regularly and consistently sending out *useful* and *valuable* insider information in the form of reports, checklists, tips, 'how-to' guides, eBooks etc., reinforces your position as the go-to expert.

Consistency is all well and good, but don't ever be tempted to send out emails just for the sake of it – to 'keep the numbers up'. Make absolutely sure each message is timely and aligned with what's happening in your subscribers' world. You will be well rewarded for it.

For example, during tough times, your audience will most likely be focused on saving money, or getting even more value for money, than ever before. Tailor your content to reflect this. Perhaps offer cost-saving tips; how to save money with bundled deals; how to cut shipping costs, etc.

Make It Easy on the Eye

Don't underestimate the power of good clean design. A visually appealing email is more likely to attract attention and get read, than a scruffy one. Use a clean, simple layout which makes your message easy to read and easy to digest. Include eye-pleasing images, strong compelling headlines, and a clear call to action.

Speaking of your *call to action* (CTA) – be certain you make it crystal clear exactly what you want your reader to do next. Is it clicking through to a blog post, redeeming a special offer, or downloading a special report or eBook? Your CTA *must* be easy to understand and clear to follow.

Test, Measure, Improve, Repeat

Email marketing has never been a case of *'set it and forget it'*. To really turbo-boost your email marketing, you must be willing to test alternative approaches, measure the impact, adjust and modify, then test again. At all times only change one thing at a time, otherwise you won't know what modification caused the change.

Experiment with subject lines, sending times, and content formats to see what resonates best with your subscribers. Track opening rates, click-through rates, and conversion rates to get a sense of how well your emails are performing. Use those insights to tweak and improve. Then test again, and again...

Maybe you'll find, for instance, emails with a personal story get more engagement than the ones without, or that your audience prefers short, punchy emails over longer, detailed ones. Whatever the case, the key is to test, test, test again. Always be learning and improving.

Summary

Email marketing may not be the newest or trendiest marketing string in your bow, but it IS one of the most effective by far. By targeting segments of your subscriber list, personalising your messages, delivering exceptional value, and staying consistent, you will build stronger relationships with your customer-base. This will help you and your business to stay top-of-mind, and the first port of call when your help is needed.

When you turbo-boost your email marketing in this way, you will be well-positioned to drive up repeat business and ride out whatever future challenges come your way.

CHAPTER 15

Emphasise Your Core Values

These days, people aren't always single-mindedly looking for just a product or service in isolation – they are also looking for a certain 'connection' – that intangible understanding where both parties are aligned in their values and beliefs.

In reality it's rarely a simple case of *what* you sell, it's also about what you and your business actually stands for. In tough times, when customers are much more selective about where they spend their money, a mutual connection of values becomes even more important.

Why?

Because people feel comfortable investing in brands and businesses they *believe* in; businesses that reflect their own values. When you clearly communicate your mission and value proposition, you give people a reason to choose you rather than one of your competitors – and to stick with you for the long term.

Start With Your 'Why'

Your *'why'* is the reason you do what you do, beyond selling products and/or services. This is the foundation of your value proposition. Is your mission to create sustainable products that help protect the planet? Do you prioritise giving back to your local community? Or maybe you are all about delivering exceptional customer service and treating every customer like family.

Whatever it is, your *'why'* is what sets you apart from the sea of mediocrity out there. It's what makes you *you*.

How to clearly communicate your *'why'*:

- Share the story of you and your business. Let people in on the journey that led to the creation of your business and why you are passionate about what you do.

- Highlight your mission statement on your website, social media, and in all your marketing materials. Make it front and centre, so it's clear to anyone who comes into contact with you.

- Show how your values influence your decisions. For example, if sustainability is important to you, talk about the measures you are taking to reduce your environmental impact, like using eco-friendly packaging or supporting green initiatives.

When you lead with your *'why'*, you invite customers into your world. You give them a reason to care about your business, beyond the products or services you offer.

Show, Don't Just Tell

It's one thing to say you stand for certain values, however it's an entirely different matter to actually *live* those values day to day in your business. Customers are savvy – they can tell if you're just paying lip service to an ideal, or are truly walking the walk.

So, don't just talk about your beliefs and values, show how you're living them *every* day. People are looking for authenticity, and they want to see you genuinely practice what you preach.

How to show your brand values in action:

> Sustainability: If you value sustainability, showcase your efforts in how you are reducing waste, sourcing ethical materials, or partnering with eco-friendly organisations. Share behind-the-scenes content that shows the steps you're taking to be environmentally conscious.
>
> Community Involvement: If giving back to the community is a core value to you, highlight your involvement in local events or charitable initiatives. Post photos of you and/or your team volunteering, or share stories about how you are supporting causes that matter the most to you.

Outstanding Customer Service: If you are renowned for going above and beyond the call of duty for your customers, let them hear it directly from those you've helped. Share testimonials, case studies and real-life examples of how you've made a difference to your customers' lives.

The key here is transparency and authenticity. Let your audience see the real impact of your values – use your blog posts, videos, social media updates, and a dedicated section on your website.

The more you can show your audience that your values and beliefs are well and truly baked into *everything* you do, the more trust and loyalty you will build.

Be Consistent Across ALL Channels

Your value proposition should never be an afterthought. Your value proposition should be tightly woven into *every* aspect of your business, from your marketing materials through to every interaction with your customers. Consistency is key here. When your values are consistently reflected in *everything* you do, it reinforces your identity and builds a deeper connection and stronger bond with your audience.

How to ensure consistency in everything you do:

Website: Make sure your values are stated clearly on your website. This can be on an 'About Us' page, a mission statement, or by highlighting specific initiatives that reflect your values. Your website should tell the story of what you stand for, as much as it promotes your products or services.

Social Media: Social media is a great platform for showcasing your values in a more personable and relatable way. Share stories, videos, and posts that reflect your values, and engage with your community in a way that aligns with your value proposition and mission statement.

Customer Support: Customer service and support should also embody your values. If one of your core values is to treat every customer like they are close family, then make sure this is evident in every thing you do and say to every one of your customers. Personalised follow-ups; attentive support; going the extra mile; all reflect your values in the way you treat your customers on a daily basis.

Consistency builds trust. In turn, trust builds loyalty. When your audience sees your values are more than just empty words; that they are a core component of who you are; they are more likely to stick with you for the long haul, through thick and thin.

Engage Your Audience in Your Mission

People love to feel they are part of something bigger. Invite your audience to join you in living your values. Whether by supporting a worthy cause, taking part in a challenge, or contributing significantly in some other way – engaging your customers in your mission will deepen their connection with you and your business.

How to engage your audience in a meaningful way:

> Social-Good Campaigns: If your values include giving back, consider launching a campaign where a percentage of your profits go to a charitable cause. Make your customers feel like they are part of the impact, by showing them the difference their custom is making.
>
> Challenges or Initiatives: Create a challenge or initiative which is in tune with your beliefs and values. Encourage your audience to get involved. For example; if sustainability is important to you, run a *'free from single-use-plastic'* challenge. Invite your customers to share their progress in this initiative on social media, or in comments on your blog posts.
>
> Encourage Conversation: Ask your customers to share their own stories. Whether it's through testimonials, social media posts, or blog comments – giving your

audience a voice helps them feel like they are part of the community you are building.

When customers become an integral and active part of your mission, they are buying into something that aligns well with their own beliefs and values. This promotes a lasting bond.

Values Build Loyalty, Even in Tough Times

In challenging times, people are more selective about where they spend their money. This is fact. They are looking for businesses that have the same values as themselves and make them feel comfortable with what they chose to buy.

Clearly communicate what you stand for, showing how you are living those values, and you hand your customers a reason to stick with you, even when the going gets tough.

It's not all about surviving an economic slump, it's also about building a strong, lasting bond and long-term loyalty. When your values resonate well with your audience, you create a deeper, emotional connection that goes way beyond any commercial transaction.

Customers who hold the same beliefs and values as you, will keep coming back, and in time become true advocates of your business, spreading the word to friends, family and colleagues.

Summary

Expressing your values is so much more than a *'nice thing to do'*, it's a powerful way of building trust, loyalty, and a lasting bond with your audience. In uncertain times, when customers are careful with their money, your values, and the things you believe in can be the differentiator that sets you apart from your competitors.

By clearly communicating what you stand for, living these values consistently, and inviting your audience to be part of your mission, will help build a business that people feel comfortable supporting, not only because of what you offer them to buy, but also because of what you passionately believe in.

CHAPTER 16

Create an Exclusive Loyalty Programme

We all like feeling we're part of something special, don't we? When times get a little bit testing, your customers will want to know they are a valued resource. They will want to feel like they are more than a mere commercial transaction. They will want a deeper connection, a stronger bond, a feeling of being *really* wanted and appreciated.

This is where an exclusive membership or a loyalty programme comes into its own.

A loyalty programme rewards your best customers and nurtures long-term relationships with them, keeping you firmly in the front of their minds.

The goal here is simple: give your very best customers a very good reason to keep coming back. Create a sense of belonging. When done right, this goes a long way to transforming casual one-off customers into loyal, lifelong advocates.

Build a Sense of Community Around Your Brand

At its core, a loyalty – or membership – programme is about fostering a sense of community. In essence, an Inner Circle or VIP Members Club is essentially where members are rewarded for their loyalty. The air of exclusivity and privilege will deepen the relationship between you and your customers, when you offer them something extra to be enthused over, beyond your products or services.

How to build community with a loyalty programme:

> Give It a Personality: Make your loyalty programme more than a transactional rewards system. Give it a name that reflects your values and tone – something that makes members feel proud to be a part of. For example; if you operate a wellness business, maybe your VIP Members become *'Wellness Warriors'*.
>
> Create a Culture: Develop a set of values, or a purpose your loyalty programme exists for. Make your members feel like they're joining a movement with a definitive goal or purpose, not just signing up for points to redeem against future purchases. This can, for instance, be linked to topics as diverse as sustainability; supporting local businesses; or living a healthier lifestyle. Create a culture that members can rally around.

Offer Special Perks, Discounts, and Exclusive Access

A loyalty programme only works if the members are getting something special out of it. This is your chance to reward your top customers' loyalty with perks they won't find anywhere else. Think beyond the basics here. Sure, discounts and redeemable points are great, but what else can you give them that makes them feel like they really are privileged?

Ideas for exclusive perks and benefits:

> Early Access to New Releases: Give your loyalty members first dibs on new product launches, before they're available to the general public, i.e. extend to them special treatment.
>
> Member-Only Discounts: Offer exclusive discounts only members can access. This can be ongoing discounts or limited-time offers giving members the very best deals, that are unavailable to non-members.
>
> Birthday Surprises: Everyone appreciates some birthday love. Send a special offer or freebie on their birthday, to show you're thinking of them on their special day.
>
> Exclusive Content: Share member-only content, such as behind-the-scenes videos; previews of upcoming projects/products; early access to blog posts or webinars, etc.

The key here is to create rewards which are meaningful and of high perceived value to your members. Your VIP members should be given access to offers and perks that are of genuine value to them. Make your members feel enthused to be part of your programme.

Make Earning Rewards Fun and Engaging

Participation in a loyalty programme should be enjoyable and engaging, to help keep your customers coming back for more. You should make earning rewards an enjoyable experience, not seen as just another step in the buying process.

How to make your loyalty programme engaging:

Points-Based System: Implement a points system where members earn points for every purchase they make. Once enough points are accumulated, they can redeem them for discounts, free products, and other goodies. Make the process easy to understand and to track, so they are always aware of how close they are to their next reward.

Bonus Points for Engagement: Reward members for making purchases, and for engaging with you in other ways. Maybe they earn extra points for leaving a review, or for sharing on social media, or by referring a friend. This creates multiple touchpoints where customers can interact with you.

Tiered Membership Levels: Introduce different membership tiers, based on spending or engagement levels. The more they spend or interact, the higher they climb. Each tier unlocks bigger and better rewards, creating an incentive to stick around and stay engaged. For example, you might have a *'Gold'* or a *'Platinum'* membership level with exclusive rewards reserved for your most loyal customers.

Make It Personal

One of the biggest advantages of a loyalty programme is the opportunity to make your customers feel seen and valued as individual people. Use the data collected from the programme to personalise their experience. After all, who doesn't appreciate a business that remembers customer preferences, celebrates their milestones, and tailors rewards especially for them?

Personalisation ideas:

Tailored Offers: Use purchasing history to offer personalised discounts on items they have shown interest in. For example; if you run a book store and a customer frequently buys mystery novels, send them a special offer on a newly released mystery title.

Custom Milestones: Create custom milestones based on how long a customer has been a member of your programme. Maybe they get a special reward on their one-year anniversary, or after they hit a specific spending threshold.

Relevant Product Recommendations: Use data from their past purchases, or website browsing behaviour, to recommend products they are likely to find useful, or enjoy. When your recommendations are relevant and thoughtful, customers are more likely to make repeat purchases.

Personalisation makes the experience feel more human. It shows your customers that you see them as people, as individuals – not just raw numbers in your sales stats.

Keep Communication Open and Engaging

A loyalty programme isn't something you set up and then forget completely about. To keep your members engaged, you need to stay in touch regularly, and in a way that's personal and engaging. This can be through email, phone calls, your social media profiles, or text messages. Be sure to communicate using the way your customers prefer, and with their express permission. Remember, you don't want to be considered as an annoying pest.

How to communicate with your members:

Regular Updates: Send regular updates to remind members of their rewards balance, upcoming member-only perks, and other exclusive offers. Keep it light, warm and friendly. Make sure they're fired-up about what's on its way down the pipeline.

Celebrate Milestones: Whether they've earned a new reward, reached a new membership tier, or just celebrated another year as a member, take the time to acknowledge this and celebrate the moment.

Engage on Social Media: Create opportunities for your members to engage with you (and each other) on social media. They could earn an extra point or two for sharing a photo of their latest purchase, or tagging your business in on a post. This builds community spirit and keeps your programme active, vibrant and relevant in members' eyes.

Remember, properly managed, regular communication with your members is essential. When members know they are a component part of an ongoing conversation, they are more likely to stay interested, engaged and active.

Make It Easy and Seamless

The best loyalty programmes are those that are easy to join, easy to understand, and easy to be part of. Don't overcomplicate things. The more seamless the experience, the more likely your customers are to stick with it.

Keeping it simple:

Easy Sign-Up: Make it simple and straightforward for customers to join your programme, e.g. via your website, email, in-store, or an opt-in opportunity at checkout.

Clear Rewards Structure: Make sure the rewards and benefits structure is clear and easy to understand. Customers should know exactly how they earn points, how to redeem them, and what member-offers they can unlock.

Seamless Redemption Process: Make it simple for members to redeem reward points, either online or in-store. Complicated processes will cause frustration. Make absolutely sure the procedure is smooth and user-friendly.

Summary

An exclusive membership, VIP club, or loyalty programme, is a powerful way to foster a deeper connection and bond with your best customers – adding another building-block to repeat business, and therefore, more sales.

By offering special member-only bonuses; personalising and customising the experience; and creating a sense of community, you are giving your most loyal customers more reasons to stick with you for longer - not only for the benefits of your range of products or services, but also for the unique experiences and added value you bring to the table through programme membership, available to members only.

CHAPTER 17

Explore Influencer Partnerships

In today's digital landscape, influencers can be likened to trusted friends with megaphones. Influencers – YouTubers, Vloggers and Bloggers – have built fiercely loyal, enthusiastic and highly engaged audiences who look to them for help, advice, recommendations, and inspiration.

Partnering with the right influencers may well open up new opportunities for you, even if working within a tight and limited budget. It's all about creating an authentic relationship which is both in-tune with their followers and also feels true to your core values and business ethos.

Influencer marketing doesn't mean you need to go straight out and spend a fortune on a celebrity endorsement. Far from it. The real magic often happens with micro-influencers – those who don't have millions of followers but nevertheless have built a tight-knit, highly engaged, enthusiastic follower community.

These micro-influencers have the potential for delivering incredible results for you, very often with more authenticity than the larger influencers. It's less about the size of their audience, and more about how engaged and active that audience is with them.

So how do you leverage influencer partnerships in a way that feels genuine, effective, and most importantly... accessible?

Let's take a look...

Find the Right Fit – Look for Alignment

When exploring influencer partnerships, the first and most important step is to find the right match. It's not necessarily about how many followers an influencer has, it's about whether their personal values and voice, are in tune with yours. Think of it like dating – you want to find someone who clicks with you, shares your vibe, and can communicate your message in a way that feels natural to them, and right for you.

Here's what to look for:

> Shared Values: Does the influencer promote values that align with the ethos and ethics of your business? If sustainability, transparency, and inclusivity are important to your business, seek out influencers who share these values and regularly talk about them.
>
> Audience Alignment: Even more important than the *number* of followers they have, is *who* those followers are. Are they in your target market? If your brand caters to parents, for example, it makes sense to partner with a

parenting influencer whose audience is made up of engaged mums and dads who wholeheartedly trust their reviews and recommendations.

Content Style: Does the influencer's content feel authentic, open, and relatable to you? Or does it feel overly polished and a bit *'salesy'*? You want someone to partner with whose style matches the voice and the tone of your brand. If you're a fun, quirky business, look for influencers who have the same playful spirit.

Remember, influencer marketing works best when it feels like a natural fit. If the partnership seems forced, or out of place, their audience will notice this, and it just won't work.

Go Small – The Power of Micro-Influencers

Micro-influencers typically have between 1,000 and 100,000 followers They are absolute gems when it comes to enthusiast engagement. Their followers are locked-in and highly attentive due to the influencer maintaining a closer, personal relationship with their followers.

Larger influencers who, without doubt, reach a much broader audience, but can struggle with targeted, relevant and meaningful engagement. Whereas micro-influencers with their smaller audiences generate greater levels of interest and engagement because of their targetted and laser-focussed content.

Why a micro-influencer partnership works better

Higher Engagement: Micro-influencers often see higher engagement rates compared to the larger ones. Their audiences are smaller yes, but more deeply engaged and fully invested in the influencer's content.

Authenticity: The micro-influencer is typically more niche and more grounded in their communities. Their recommendations are credible and carry weight because their followers see them as trusted sources who don't promote something just for the sake of it.

Budget-Friendly: Micro-influencers are far more cost-effective than their macro and celebrity counterparts. Many are happy to collaborate in exchange for complimentary products, experiences, or for a small fee.

The key to success with micro-influencers is finding those who genuinely love and appreciate your product or service, and are excited to share it with their followers. Their authenticity and enthusiasm shines through. Also, their followers easily sense when the influencer they follow is truly fired-up and passionate about something.

Build Authentic Collaborations

Once you've found the right influencers for you, the next step is to build a relationship that feels real, genuine and of mutual benefit, i.e. you're not just paying for one or two posts. The best influencer partnerships are built on trust, creativity, and mutually beneficial collaboration. It's about working together to create content that is seen and perceived as genuine, authentic and of value to their followers.

Creating meaningful collaborations:

Give Creative Freedom: Influencers know their audiences better than you do. Trust them to create content that feels true to their style. Instead of giving them strict rules or scripting every detail, let them tell it in a way that resonates with their followers. This makes their content natural and not feel like a forced ad.

Collaborate on Content: Work together as a partnership to create content. This can be anything from a product review, or an unboxing video, to a behind-the-scenes look at the way your business does things. Whatever the format, make sure the content speaks to their audience in a way that comes over as real and relates to what they consider as important in their lives.

Focus on Storytelling: Instead of just asking an influencer to say, *'Buy this product'*, think about how you can use their platform to tell a compelling story about your product. Maybe it's about how it can solve a specific problem in their life or make their daily routine easier. Relate a few customer experiences also. When influencers can tie your product to a personal experience, it becomes real.

Remember, influencers are content creators at heart. Let them be creative, and you'll likely see better results, since the content will resonate more readily with their audience.

Create Long-Term Partnerships

While one-off posts can work well, creating long-term partnerships is when you'll reap the greatest reward. Building an ongoing relationship with an influencer has the effect of increasing the credibility of their recommendations.

Their audience will see that they truly believe in your product and also trust you as a professional business person who supplies high quality products and services, proven to be of great benefit to the same kind of people as their followers.

Benefits of long-term partnerships:

Building Trust: The more an influencer talks about you, your business, and your products, the more their followers will trust what they are seeing and hearing as something worth paying attention to.

A one-off product recommendation might be enough to convince a few to consider looking into things a bit further, whereas seeing and hearing it repeatedly from someone they trust? This is pure gold.

Deeper Engagement: Within a long-term partnership arrangement, influencers can integrate your brand into different types of content, using a variety of media – this could be in a blog, social media posts, or in YouTube videos. This mixing of media-types places you in front of their followers more often, and in more places.

Consistency: Consistent, regular exposure over time leads to better recall. When influencer followers are in the market for a product like yours, they will more than likely think of you first. Why? Because they've seen the product reviewed and recommended so often by someone they know and trust.

Long-term partnerships also allow you to build a stronger relationship with the influencer, with the potential to lead to further collaborative projects.

Track Results, Stay Flexible

As with any marketing strategy you put to work, it's vitally important to measure the results of your influencer partnerships. Keep track of key metrics such as engagement rates, referral traffic, and conversions. If certain types of content or partnerships perform better than others, be flexible, modify and adjust your approach.

Metrics to track:

> Engagement Rates: How are followers interacting with the influencer's content? Are they liking, commenting, sharing, asking questions about your product or service?
>
> Referral Traffic: If you're working with an influencer primarily to drive traffic to your website, track how many visitors are arriving from a link in their posts, or videos.
>
> Conversions: Did the influencer's campaign result in any actual sales, or sign-ups? This is a key metric to determine the return-on-investment of your partnership. Adjust as necessary.

And don't forget – influencer marketing is all about testing, testing, and more testing. Some partnerships will work better than others. Be open to trying new things and adjusting your strategy based on what works best and ultimately, what approach proves more profitable for you.

Keeping It Genuine

At the end of the day, influencer marketing is all about authenticity. The more genuine your partnerships feel, the more likely they will succeed.

It's certainly nothing about finding someone to 'shill' your products or services – it's about building professional, meaningful, quality relationships with influencers who align with your type of business and products and connect with their followers from a position of trust.

Summary

Influencer partnerships are an incredibly effective way of expanding your reach, even if you're running a tight budget. The key is finding the right influencers for you. Influencers whose values reflect those of yours, and those you can work together with to create promotional content that presents as genuine and authentic, as well as engaging and meaningful.

Whether your choice is for just a one-time post, or a longer term collaboration, the goal in either case is to build trust and credibility with their followers. When done right, influencer marketing builds a community around your brand. In other words, an enthusiastic fan base.

CHAPTER 18

Go Hyper-Local

In times of economic uncertainty, people instinctively gravitate towards that which is closer to home. They tend to look to their local communities for support. As a business, this is a fantastic opportunity for you to strengthen your ties with the locals.

By adopting a hyper-local marketing approach, you can build stronger relationships with customers in your immediate neighbourhood – those who are eager to support businesses which are part of their own community.

'Buy Local' is a slogan often seen, encouraging communities to support their local businesses.

Hyper-local marketing is not only being *geographically* close to your audience, it's also being close *emotionally*. It's about showing you are heavily invested in the same community they also care deeply about. And don't forget, if you're going hyper-local, your success is tied inextricably to the well-being of the local ecosystem.

Let's break it down into actionable steps that can make going hyper-local a powerful contributor to the on-going growth of your business...

Participate in Local Events and Good Causes

One of the best ways to connect with your local community is to be visible in the places they care about – both physically and virtually. Whether it's sponsoring a local charity run, participating in a neighbourhood festival, or donating to a community cause - these small actions have a big impact and build goodwill.

When your business is actively involved in the community, people begin to see you as an integral part of the community. This connection matters a great deal, especially in tough times when people are more likely to support businesses they see as positively contributing to the local area.

> Sponsor Local Events: From school fundraisers to farmers' markets – actively seek out local events and *get involved*. Sponsorship doesn't always have to be a financial arrangement, it can also be in-kind donations of products or services, or even your time as a volunteer.
>
> Host Community-Focused Events: Why not host a workshop or class, that directly serves local people? Think of it as a way of giving back, building relationships,

and showcasing your expertise. In this way, you will get to be recognised as the local go-to expert.

Support Local Causes: Consider donating a percentage of your profits to a community organisation or charity, or help to promote a local cause on your website or social media accounts. People will appreciate seeing your total commitment to the same things they care about in their local community.

Being present at community events positions you and your business as a trusted partner – someone who is just as invested in the success of the neighbourhood as the residents are.

Highlight Local Suppliers and Partnerships

One way to stand out in a crowded market is to emphasise your commitment to building local connections. Customers are happy supporting businesses that keep their hard-earned cash circulating within the community. Highlighting your local suppliers; local partners (and even employees) differentiates you from the rest, in a clear, distinct and meaningful way.

When you showcase your local suppliers, you're not just selling a product or service – you're now also relating a story. People want to know where the products they buy come from, who made them, and how their purchase impacts the local economy. Highlighting these elements brings a whole new level of credibility and trust to your business.

Ideas for highlighting local connections:

Share Local Suppliers' Stories: If you partner with local small businesses, shine a spotlight on these partnerships in all your marketing materials. Tell their stories through blog posts, social media, and videos. It shows your customers you are committed to supporting other local small businesses.

Feature Local Collaborations: If you've teamed up with local businesses for joint promotions or products, highlight these collaborations. Customers love to know local businesses are working together and supporting each other.

Showcase Local Employees: If your team is made up of local talent, make sure to introduce them through your marketing. People are often curious about the people behind a business. Showing off the faces and personalities of your team will humanise your business and create a sense of community connection. And don't forget to introduce your team on your website.

Use Geo-Targeted Ads

The power of digital marketing lies in its ability to get your message in front of the right people at the right time. For a hyper-local approach, you can use geo-targeted ads to zero-in on potential customers in your local area. These kind of ads allow you to deliver location-specific messages that feel more relevant and personalised to your local audience.

Imagine being able to promote a special sale or event to people within a 10-mile radius of your shop or service area. With geo-targeted ads on platforms like Google and Facebook, you can do just that – making sure your message reaches those most likely to stop by or take advantage of a local offer.

How to leverage geo-targeted ads:

> Promote In-Store Events or Offers: If you're running a special promotion, sale, or other event at your physical location, use geo-targeted ads to promote it to the nearby audience. Include enticing offers such as *'10% discount for local residents'* to encourage an increase in foot-fall.
>
> Highlight Local Relevance: Tailor your ad copy to speak to the *specific* needs of your local audience. For example; if you're a local HVAC company and the weather is turning colder, geo-target your ads to promote heating products and services to residents in your immediate locality. Make it feel personal and relevant to their immediate concerns and worries.
>
> Boost Visibility on Local Searches: Make sure you are optimising for local search on Google. People in your area searching for products or services like yours should

see *you* first, and geo-targeted ads will help ensure that happens.

Geo-targeted ads give you the ability to speak directly to your local audience with messages that are personal and timely, and so driving more traffic and interest from those located closest to you.

Tailor Messaging to the Local Community

When you are speaking to a local audience, the messages you put out should reflect that at all times. Use language, references, and examples that the local community can relate to. The more your messages are personalised to the locals within your area, the more people will feel you are one of them.

Incorporate local landmarks, traditions, or events into your social media posts, newsletters, and other marketing materials. Show you are not yet another faceless business – you are an integral part of the community, and you understand why it's special.

How to personalise your message:

Reference Local Landmarks or Traditions: Whether it's a beloved coffee shop down the road, or a county fair, or the annual carnival, by incorporating local culture into your content your marketing will come over as in-tune, pertinent, and personal.

Acknowledge Local Challenges: If your community is going through a tough time (for example, recovering from a natural disaster or navigating severe economic challenges), acknowledge this in your messaging, and offer ways you are able to help support the community.

Create Community-Centred Content: Think about putting out blog posts, social media content, and newsletters that focus solely on topics important to the local community. Whether it's a guide to local events, or tips for supporting other local businesses – this kind of content firmly positions your business as a trusted resource for all things local.

By carefully tailoring your message to speak directly to the heart of your local community, you create a stronger emotional connection with your audience – one that goes well beyond any commercial transaction. Embrace this approach. It's powerful.

Summary

Going hyper-local is a highly effective way to deepen the connection with your customers by showing you are part of the very same community they know, love, and care deeply about.

By participating in local events, highlighting local partnerships, using geo-targeted ads, and personalising your messaging, you build trust, credibility, loyalty, and a close engagement with those in your local area. These local connections will become your strongest asset, helping your business grow and thrive by creating genuine, supportive and lasting relationships with local residents.

CHAPTER 19

Tap into Video Marketing

There is *one* thing that has dominated centre stage in today's content creation landscape, and that's *video*. Video marketing isn't limited for big-budget corporations like it used to be. Thanks to platforms like Instagram, YouTube, and TikTok, video has become the most engaging, accessible, and dynamic form of marketing content that *anyone* can create and share, regardless of budget.

The best part is, you don't need a fancy camera, production crew, or film director to make video work really well for you. With just your phone, a lapel mic, and a bit of creative thinking, you too can tap into the immense power of video marketing.

Here's how...

Keep It Short, Sweet and Engaging

The beauty of video marketing is that it allows you to pack a whole lot of punch into just a short amount of time. In today's fast-paced digital world, people often don't have time for long, drawn-out narratives. For this reason, focus on creating short, bite-sized videos which deliver great value *quickly*. Whether you're showcasing a product, offering tips, or sharing a behind-the-scenes look into your business, keeping your videos relevant and concise ensures your audience stays with you.

Aim for videos that are anywhere from 30 seconds to 2 minutes long. Think of them as snackable content – easy for your audience to consume and digest quickly, without taking up too much of their time.

How to get started with video:

Product Demos: Create short videos highlighting the benefits of your products to your viewers or, better still, demonstrate how they work. Show them in action and emphasise the benefits. Selling by demonstration is an extremely effective approach to adopt. Incorporate it in your marketing as often as you can.

'How-To' Videos: Educational content is a big hit with people these days. Whether you're demonstrating how to use a product to its very best advantage, or sharing related hints, tips, and insider tricks, *'how-to'* videos are a powerful way of delivering great value.

Behind-The-Scenes: People like to see the real, human side of a business. So take them behind the scenes, take them on a tour to show them how your day-to-day operations work. Perhaps interview one or two of your staff. Post the video on your YouTube channel, and in social media feeds.

Keep your videos short, sweet and engaging. Make them easy to watch so hold your viewers' interest from start to finish.

Focus on Reality, Rather Than Perfection

Your videos do not need to be perfect. In fact, raw authenticity wins out every time over polish. People today value content that comes over as real and relatable. In other words, something that speaks to them in simple language on a personal level, rather than a highly-produced info-commercial that sounds and looks scripted and staged.

With just a smartphone and a very basic setup, you can create videos that feel intimate, genuine, and engaging. Don't stress over perfect lighting or having a professional backdrop. Your audience will connect more with the raw, unfiltered side of your business, as opposed to a super-polished production.

How to embrace authenticity:

Be Yourself: Don't worry to much about being 'camera-ready'. Speak naturally, smile, show your personality. If you fumble a word or two, who cares? It doesn't matter. It makes you more personable.

Use Simple Equipment: You don't need expensive gear. A phone camera, a tripod or phone stand, and a lapel mic are all you need to start creating really good video content. If natural light is available, use it to brighten things up a bit. If not, don't worry. Simple setups still produce great results.

Show the Real Behind-the-Scenes: Share the day-to-day reality of your business. If you're packing up orders, working in the shop, or chatting with your team, show that reality. People want to see the real stuff, the human side of your business Video is the perfect way to do that.

Remember, the more authentic and true-to-life your videos feel, the more likely your audience will warm to you, and listen to your message.

Share Your Story Through Video

Video is the ultimate storytelling tool. Video storytelling gives you a great opportunity to connect emotionally with your viewers by letting them see, hear, and experience you and your business in a way that words alone just can't manage.

Create videos to share your story. Share the journey you've been on. Share the challenges you've overcome. Share your values, your goals and the mission that drives you and your business forward. Explain how your life experiences can benefit your viewers, when they become customers. People enjoy a good tale, especially one they can relate to and one which also shows realistic ways they can make their lives better, happier, less stressful, more comfortable.

By showing how your story can benefit your viewers in some way, you're creating a bond that fosters trust, builds credibility, and promotes loyalty.

What to include in your storytelling videos:

> Your Origin: How did your business come into being? What problem were you trying to solve at the time? Why are you passionate about what you do? In what ways can you now help your viewers, as a result of the journey you've been on? Share this all with your audience – it humanises your business.
>
> Your Values and Mission: What do you stand for? What values drive your business? Is it sustainability, people's health and wellbeing, or technology and innovation? Use video to communicate why and how your values are riveted to the core of your business model.
>
> Customer Experiences: If your customers have had great successes or experiences with your product that they would like to share, give them the opportunity to tell all on camera. This highlights the intrinsic value of your products and also demonstrates first-hand, real life results people are benefitting from.

By using video to tell your story, you build a personal connection with your audience that goes beyond just selling a product. It creates a narrative that draws people to you, making them feel part of your journey.

Leverage Social Media to Share Your Videos

Once you've created your video content, it's time to get it out there into the world. Social media is one of the best platforms for sharing video content. It allows you to reach a large audience. It's where your customers and prospective customers are already hanging out and spending time.

Each platform offers different video formats and opportunities:

Instagram: Use Instagram Stories, Reels, or IGTV to share short videos. Reels, in particular, are ideal for quick, creative content that can easily go viral.

Facebook: Facebook allows for longer-form videos which you can share directly on your page or in groups. You can also use Facebook Live to broadcast real-time events.

YouTube: As the second largest search engine in the world, YouTube is the best place for educational and *'how-to'* videos. If you're producing videos that offer value over time, such as tutorials or deep dives, this is the platform to choose.

TikTok: If you target a younger market, TikTok is a great platform for short, fun, and creative videos that can quickly engage with a highly active and motivated audience.

The key here is to tailor and fine-tune your video content to each platform and audience. Short, engaging videos tend to perform best on social media, while longer, more in-depth videos work well on YouTube.

Integrate Video into Your Email Marketing

Video can be a powerful addition to your email marketing campaigns, helping you connect with your audience in a more dynamic way. A well-placed video can increase engagement, boost click-through rates, and provide a more interactive experience for your subscribers.

Whether you're announcing a new product, sharing a tutorial, or simply checking in with your subscribers, embedding a short video in your email is an effective way to grab attention and convey your message. Make sure to include a compelling thumbnail or animated GIF to entice people to click and watch.

Ideas for video in email marketing:

Product Launch: Share the excitement and enthusiasm of a new product launch with a compelling video to showcase key features and the major benefits.

Tutorials or Demos: Include instructional videos to help customers get the most out of your products.

Personal Messages: A personalised video greeting or 'thank-you' message to your email list helps to strengthen a personal connection to your subscribers.

Summary

Video marketing is by no means complex or expensive. Start with the basics. Keep your videos short. Focus on being authentic. Use simple tools like your phone and a lapel mic. Share your videos across social media, email, and your website to engage your audience.

By tapping into the marketing power of video, you can create a strong bond with your audience; relate your story in an engaging way; and ultimately stand out from the crowd. And remember, video need not be absolutely perfect to be effective. Authenticity, relatability, and consistency are the keys to making video marketing work well for you.

CHAPTER 20

Streamline Your Offerings

When customers are tightening their wallets and being more selective about where they spend their money, *simplicity* is your secret weapon. Too many choices can overwhelm people. It's like walking into a crowded farmers' market and feeling confused because every stall holder is shouting for your attention.

By streamlining your offerings, you're cutting through the noise and making it easier for your customers to find exactly what they are looking for – quickly and confidently. The goal here is to reduce *'decision fatigue'*. Focus on your top-performing products or services, and make the buying process as easy and as straightforward as possible.

Streamlining will help you stand out and make your business the obvious choice for cautious customers.

Focus on Your Best Sellers

Think of your product or service line-up like a restaurant menu; if it's too long, it becomes overwhelming. Too much information only leads to greater confusion. The key is to focus on your best-sellers. These are the items that appeal and resonate most with your customers and, as a result, sell more and drive the highest profit into your business.

Start by looking at your sales data. What are your top-performing products or services? These are the items your customers really like, so why not make them the star of the show?

By narrowing your focus to your most popular items, you can hone and sharpen your message to offer your audience fewer, and much more impactful choices.

Review Your Sales Data: Analyse which products or services are generating the most profit. These should be in the front and centre of all your marketing.

Customer Feedback: What do your customers rave about most in their reviews and testimonials? Listen to what they are saying and focus in on the benefits and results your customers are experiencing and enthusing over.

Cut the Clutter: If there are products that really aren't pulling their weight, seriously consider removing them. Take them out of the picture completely. Less is more when it comes to presenting customers with clear and simple choices.

By doubling down on your best-performing line-items, you are simplifying and streamlining your customers' decision-making process. You are making it easier for them to appreciate the intrinsic value in your products or services. As a result, making it easier for them to reach that all-important decision to buy.

Simplify the Decision-Making Process

When people are more cautious with their spending, they need to feel certain they are making the right decision. They need to be guided towards the right decision, step-by-step. Simplifying their options is a great way to do this and reduce friction in the buying process. Too many choices can lead to *'analysis paralysis'*, where your customers can get stuck weighing up too many options and end up leaving without making any decision at all.

The answer is to offer a curated selection of your best selling products, or services, with clear descriptions highlighting the benefits and the results people will enjoy once they buy.

This not only makes it easier for people to make a wise and informed choice, but also signals that you understand their needs, wants and desires, and have already done the hard work of narrowing down the best options for them.

Streamlining suggestions:

Create Clear Product Categories: Organise your line up into easy-to-understand product categories, or service tiers, so customers can quickly and easily find what they are looking for.

Highlight Key Benefits: Use simple, benefit-focused language to explain what each product or service will do for your customer and how it will solve their problem.

Reduce Overwhelm: If you have a lot of similar offerings, consider bundling them together into fewer packages. This simplifies the choices available, helping to avoid your customers' becoming overwhelmed and confused, leading to a lost sale.

By simplifying the decision-making process, you create a smoother path leading to a quicker purchase. Less steps in the process means less effort expected of your customer, which in turn, means more sales for you.

Bundle for Value

Bundling is a powerful way to streamline, while giving your customers greater value for their money. By combining complementary products or services into one package, you will create a sense of added-value without confusing your customers with too many choices.

Bundles are especially effective because they:

Simplify Choices: Instead of buying lots of items individually, customers can choose a pre-curated package that gives them what they want, all at once.

Encourage Larger Purchases: Bundling can increase the average value of a sale by offering an appealing deal that feels too good to pass up.

Offer Savings: Even if the discount is small, people feel good about getting more for less with a bundle of products, over buying each one individually.

Examples of bundling:

Product Bundles: If you sell physical products, consider bundling complementary items together. For example; if you're a skincare product supplier, create a bundle of a cleanser, moisturiser, and sunscreen. Offer the bundle at a slightly discounted price compared to buying each item one by one.

Service Packages: If you offer services, bundle them into packages which provide a higher value. For example, a digital marketing agency might offer a *'starter pack'* that includes website audits, SEO, and a social media strategy – making it easier for customers to get everything they were looking for, all in one go.

Tiered Pricing: Again, for services, offer tiered packages where each level provides more value than the previous one. In this way, customers can choose the package that best fits their budget and requirements, without feeling overwhelmed by too many options.

Bundles not only streamline the buying process they also give customers a feeling of receiving more value for their money - a key factor when they are being more cautious with spending.

Offer Simplified Service Packages

If you run a service business, streamlining doesn't mean cutting corners or trimming back on your level of service – it's more about making your offerings easier to understand and easily accessible. Instead of offering a long list of custom designed services, create clear, simplified packages that deliver exactly what your customers want, without any fuss.

Why simplified service packages will work so well for you:

Easy to Understand: Customers can quickly see what is included and how much it costs, without needing a lengthy consultation or complex pricing breakdown.

Save Time: Simplified packages reduce back-and-forth communication and make it easier for customers to choose the right service for them, in a timely manner.

Appeal to Budget-Conscious Buyers: Offering a range of price points, from entry-level to premium, gives customers the flexibility to choose a package that fits their budget without feeling overwhelmed by endless custom variations.

How to create service packages:

Bundle Common Services: Group popular services together into easy-to-purchase packages. For example; if you're a consultant, create a *'starter'* pack which includes an initial consultation, an audit, and an actionable report.

Tier your offerings: Offer multiple levels of service packages, from basic to premium, so customers can choose what fits their budget and requirements. Make it clear what is included at each level and the added benefits of upgrading to the next.

Provide clear pricing: Avoid a complex pricing structure. Simplify it so customers can easily understand what they are paying for. Also make sure they understand the great value they are getting for their money. Important at any time, and especially important during an economic slow down.

By offering simplified service packages, you reduce confusion and so create a clearer path towards a positive purchasing decision.

Promote Your Streamlined Offerings

Once you've completed streamlining your offerings, it's time to shout about them from the hill tops. Make sure your audience knows about the simplicity, the value, and the ease you've built into your product or service line-up. In all your marketing materials and channels, emphasise how your streamlined offerings save time, reduce hassle, and offer more value than ever before.

How to promote your streamlined offerings:

Update Your Website: Make sure your website reflects the simplified line-up, with clear, easy-to-navigate, easy-to-read pages that showcase your streamlined offerings front and centre.

Social Media: Use your social media profiles to announce your new streamlined line-up. Highlight the benefits and the results. Share behind-the-scenes insights into why you've simplified things. Encourage your audience to check out your new look line-up.

Email Campaigns: Send targeted emails to your subscriber list. Let them know about your simplified product or service bundles, and new packages. Emphasise how these changes make it easier (and more affordable) for them to get the great value they are searching for from your business.

Summary

Streamlining during an economic slowdown makes it far easier for your customers to buy from you. Streamlining also demonstrates you understand your customers' needs, wants and desires and that you are 100% committed to helping them make wise, informed, and value-driven buying decisions.

By focusing on what works best for them, bundling for value, and offering clear, simplified choices, you create a customer experience that's efficient, satisfying, and in-tune with a cautious mindset.

In uncertain times, less really can be more. By cutting through the clutter, you will be able to position your business as the easy, no-brainer choice for those who crave clarity and simplicity in their purchases.

CHAPTER 21

Stay Consistent and Visible

One of the most powerful business growth tools you have available to you is *consistency*. It's easy to get swept up in the chaos of shifting markets, changing customer behaviours, and economic downturns. But when your business stays *visible, solid and dependable*, you become a beacon of reliability in the eyes of your customers.

People gravitate toward what feels familiar and secure. Showing up regularly and consistently, will foster a sense of stability.

Consistency is not always about how *often* you post on social media or how often you send out emails to your list of subscribers – it's also about the *message*, the *tone*, and the *value* you deliver each and every time you're seen.

Build Trust Through Repetition

Consistency builds trust. It's as simple as that. When you turn up regularly in your customers' inboxes, on social media feeds, or at community events, you become a familiar and reliable presence. Think of it like building a friendship. It's the regular check-ins, the small interactions, and the ongoing conversations that strengthen the relationship over time.

In a world where uncertainty can breed anxiety, people want to know they can count on your business. By being ever-present and consistent, you are sending the message – *'We're still here. We're still delivering value to you. We're still committed to you.'*

3 top ways of building trust through consistency:

Post Regularly: Whether it's on social media, your website blog, or through email, stick to a consistent schedule. If you post a new blog on a Tuesday, or send out an email Tuesday mornings, make sure you repeat *every* Tuesday.

Maintain Your Tone and Voice: Be consistent in the way you communicate. Your tone should reflect your personality. Customers should feel like they are interacting with the same person every time, whether they are reading your emails, your blog posts, or your social media updates.

Stick to Your Values: Reinforce your values through your content and actions. People trust businesses that consistently reflect their core values. Don't stray from what your business stands for, just because times have become tougher.

The more consistently you show up, the more customers begin to associate your business with reliability and stability – two qualities people are always searching for.

Deliver Valuable Content on a Reliable Schedule

Consistency in marketing doesn't just mean frequency. It also means delivering value at the right time, over and over again. If your customers can count on you to show up with helpful, insightful, and actionable content, they are more likely to stay with you – even when they're being cautious with their budgets.

People have busy lives. When they see your email in their inbox, or your post on social media, they should immediately know it's going to be worth their time reading it. This is how you keep them coming back for more, and this is how you stay top-of-mind when they are ready to buy.

How to stay consistent with content:

> Stick to a Schedule: If you promise a weekly newsletter, deliver it every week without fail. If you're posting on Instagram three times a week, keep that pace up. The goal is for your audience to know when to expect your content, and to anticipate it.
>
> Be Predictable in Your Value: Customers should know what kind of value to expect from you. Whether you're sharing *'how-to'* guides, market-sector insights, or

exclusive deals, make sure your content consistently aligns with your value proposition.

Create a Content Calendar: Planning ahead is key to maintaining consistency. Develop a content calendar to map out your blog posts, social media updates, and email campaigns in advance, so you are never scrambling for ideas at the last minute.

Delivering consistent value not only strengthens your relationship with your audience but also establishes your business as a reliable source of information and expertise.

Be Consistent in Customer Engagement

Beyond content, consistency in the *way* you engage with your customers is essential. They could be reaching out to you through social media, email, or customer service channels. The way you respond – and how *quickly* you respond – reflects your level of professionalism.

During uncertain times, customers need reassurance. They need to know that if they have a problem or a question, you'll be there to help, and you'll respond in a timely, helpful and supportive manner. Consistency in the way you engage with your customers differentiates your business from all the others, and also builds long-term loyalty.

How to ensure consistent customer engagement:

Respond Quickly: Set clear goals for how quickly you will respond to customer inquiries and stick to them. Even if you don't have the full solution immediately, let them know you will get back to them within a specific time period, and stick rigidly to it. Even if you haven't found a solution yet, tell them that. People can deal with bad news, they don't cope well with no news. Don't ever go quiet on them.

Use Consistent Messaging: Whether it's through social media comments, email replies, or a simple phone call, the interaction with your customers should reflect the same tone, values and ethos, as the rest of your marketing and promotional materials. Customers should feel confident they are interacting with the very same business they initially came into contact with, as they are on all subsequent contact, no matter what the platform.

Follow Through: Consistency also means *doing* what you *say* you will do. If you promise a follow-up, deliver it without fail. If you say a product will be restocked at a certain date, restock it on or before that date. Following through and delivering on your promises is absolutely critical. It reinforces trust and reliability.

We all remember the businesses that consistently deliver exceptional customer service without fail, don't we? We also remember those that don't, just as well – the businesses that give consistently bad customer service, if any at all. Sadly, in my experience, these are in the majority. Don't be one of them. Shine through like a lighthouse in the fog.

When customers know they can rely on your business to deliver consistently – whether that be through the quality of your products, services, content, or customer support – you'll stand out as a business that cares and is set for the long haul, not just here for the quick sale.

Stay Visible, Even When The Going Gets Tough

It can be tempting to scale back when times are beginning to get a bit rougher. However, staying visible consistently – especially as others are tending to shrink back – is what will keep your business seen standing proud above the parapet, and eminently memorable because of that.

Out of sight, out of mind can quickly become a stark reality if you stop communicating with your customers and prospects. Even if your budget is tight, maintaining a regular presence in the minds of your target market really does make a difference to your future growth.

How to stay constantly visible without over-extending yourself:

> Leverage Low-Cost Channels: Social media and email marketing are the most cost-effective ways to stay in

touch with your audience. There is no need to invest heavily in paid advertising. Regular messaging and posting works just as well, if not better in some cases.

Be Active in Your Community: Online forums, industry groups, business networking, and other local events all help you stay engaged with your community. This helps you maintain a consistent presence and shows your business is alive and active, even if you're not launching new products or services every single month.

Keep Your Website Updated: Make sure your website is up-to-date with your latest offerings, content, and news. Visitors and browsers should immediately see your business is active and busy and you are still providing value, in the way of useful and informative blog posts and articles. Also offer a free download of a guide, a checklist, or tips booklet, relevant to your target market.

By consistently *'being there'* even during the more difficult times, you are reminding your customers you are still around… you are stable, committed, and trustworthy – qualities that will keep them coming back to you, time after time.

Consistency Builds Long-Term Loyalty

In the long run, consistency is about more than just staying visible. It's about building loyalty. Customers are more likely to stick with businesses they trust. Trust builds from repeated positive experiences. By consistently delivering value, engaging with your customers, and maintaining your tone, your values and your message, you will not just stay afloat during difficult times, you will be laying solid foundations for guaranteed long-term growth and success.

How to foster long-term loyalty:

Reinforce Your Identity: Every contact your customer has with your business should at all times reinforce your identity, your philosophy, and your values. This helps build and maintain a strong connection between you and your customer.

Create Predictable Experiences: When customers know what to expect from you, they are more likely to keep coming back as a repeat customer. Consistent service, quality, and communications create a sense of security and trust which ultimately leads to repeat business.

Reward Loyalty: Consistently reward your loyal customers. Whether it's through a loyalty programme, exclusive deals, or simply acknowledging them with a simple *'thank-you'*, shows appreciation for their continued custom and support. These little things, make a huge difference.

In the end, consistency is about *'being there'* for your customers when they need you most. Whether that's through content, engagement, or level of support and service – the businesses which stay visible, dependable, and valuable *consistently* are the ones that not only survive but truly thrive during tough times, and well beyond.

Summary

Remaining steadfastly consistent in ALL you do, is one of the most powerful business growth strategies you can adopt. Consistency builds trust, reinforces reliability, and keeps your business top-of-mind with your customers.

Whether it's through regular useful content, unbeatable customer support and after-sales service, or community engagement – showing up regularly, even in small ways, sends out a rock solid message of stability, commitment and reliability.

Remember, being consistent doesn't mean being perfect. You will never achieve perfection in anything you do, so stop trying. Consistency means being available at all times when customers need you; delivering value to your customers when they ask for it it; and building a relationship based on trust and reliability for everyone you and your business comes into contact with.

When you show up; when you are right there; when you are consistently visible; when you haven't shrunk into your shell because things are getting a bit difficult – your audience, your prospects and your customers WILL notice. Only really good things will ever come out of that.

Wait, there's more...

BONUS CHAPTER 1

Lean into Community

When the road ahead looks like it's going to get bumpier, there's nothing more comforting than knowing you're not travelling it alone. This is exactly why community connection matters so much. It's where people find support, share experiences, and build relationships that make everything feel a little less daunting.

Community is More Important Than Ever

In uncertain times, people naturally seek out connections that make them feel wanted, understood and supported. They want to belong to something bigger than themselves – a community where they can find comfort, share stories, and navigate challenges together. As a small business owner or, solopreneur, you have a unique opportunity to create that space for your customers.

Building a community around your business isn't about driving sales (though that can certainly be a happy by-product). It's more about fostering a sense of *'belonging'*, where your customers feel like they are part of something bigger, meaningful, and of tangible value to them. It's about giving them a place where they can connect with you, with each other, and with the values your business stands for.

Creating Space for Connection

So how exactly do you *'lean into community'* and create a virtual space where your customers feel engaged and supported? It starts with creating opportunities for connection - whether that's a digital space like a Facebook group, a forum on your website, or a regular online meetup on Zoom.

Let's take a deeper look:

> Facebook Groups: A Facebook group is an incredible tool for building a community. It's a space where your customers can interact with you and with each other. You can use it to share updates, ask questions, and get conversations going. What makes it really special is the sense of camaraderie that can develop among members. When people start engaging with each other – sharing tips, offering support, or just chatting about their day – is when you know you have built something really useful and meaningful.
>
> Website Forum: If you prefer to keep things a little closer to home, consider adding a forum to your website. This can be a dedicated space where your customers can start discussions, ask questions, and share experiences. A

forum keeps the conversation right there on your website, which in turn drives more traffic to it. Google prefers active websites and tends to rank them higher in search results.

Online Meetups: Another great way to foster a community spirit is through regular online meetups. These can be live events like webinars, Q&A sessions, or casual hangouts where people can connect in real-time. The key here is consistency (where have you heard that before?). Schedule the meetups regularly so your community knows when to log in. A reminder email, with joining details is essential if you are hosting Zoom meetings. It's very much like hosting a small party where everyone who shows up is there because they care about how everyone is and what they are doing.

Engage and Encourage Participation

Once you've created your community space, the next step is to engage actively. This isn't just about posting stuff then walking away, it's about being present, asking questions, encouraging feedback, and genuinely listening to what your community has to say.

Ask Questions: Get the conversation started by asking open-ended questions to invite your community members to share their thoughts, experiences, or ideas. Start your questions with *'How...', 'Why...', 'What...'*

'Where...'. Your questions don't always have to be directly related to your products or services. Sometimes, asking about broader topics – like what challenges people are facing, what inspires them, or how are they coping with current events – can lead to deeper, more insightful conversations.

Share Insights: Don't be afraid to share your own insights also - such as advice based on your experience and expertise, or lessons learned from your own journey, or something interesting you've recently come across. Sharing valuable information and insights positions you as a trusted resource. It shows you are invested in, and committed to, providing real value for people – not just promoting your business – which wouldn't go down very well in any case.

Encourage Sharing: One of the most powerful aspects of a community group is the shared experiences of its members. Encourage people to share their own experiences, tips, hints and advice with the group. Highlight user-generated content, celebrate their successes, and make them feel like they are an integral part of the community. When people are seen to be appreciated, they are more likely to stay engaged and contribute more to the group.

The Power of Community

When you *'lean into community'*, you will be growing a group of people who are already customers, as well as prospective customers, plus those who have shown an interest in you and your business but yet to buy. At the same time, you are creating a network of advocates who feel personally connected to you and your business. In tough times, this sense of community and belonging is incredibly powerful.

> Support: A strong community offers support, from you, and from fellow members. When your customers know they can turn to your community for advice, encouragement, or a friendly chat, it creates a bond that goes way beyond a simple business transaction.
>
> Loyalty: Community fosters loyalty. When people feel they are part of something worthwhile, they are more likely to stick around. They are more likely to choose your products or services over any other, even when money is tight. Why? Because they feel they have a connection with you and with what you are offering as a solution, which is not too common these days, when people are far too flustered to pass the time of day sometimes.
>
> Advocacy: Finally, a thriving community turns satisfied customers into advocates. They will talk about your business enthusiastically, highly recommend your products or services, and bring others into the fold.

Word-of-mouth marketing is incredibly powerful. It all starts with building a strong and engaged community. Embrace it.

Summary

Leaning into community is principally about creating a space, often virtually. It's about nurturing a sense of belonging and a connection that resonates with your customers on a deeper level than any pure business transaction can muster.

It's about making yourself available, facilitating conversations, and making sure they know they are not alone. By doing this, you are actively supporting your customers. You are creating a loyal and engaged community who will stand by you and your business through thick and thin.

BONUS CHAPTER 2

Share Customer Successes

When it comes to building trust and credibility, there's nothing quite as powerful as a real success story from someone who's *'been there and done that'*. It's one thing for *you* to say your product or service is great, but when your customers say it for you? That's solid gold. Customer stories of their findings, results and experiences when using your products or services are so much more than testimonials, they are living proof that your business actually delivers on its promises.

Why Are Customer Success Stories Important?

In unsettling times, everyone is craving for stability and reassurance. Potential customers want to be assured they are making the right choice – that their hard-earned money is going towards something that will truly make a beneficial difference to their lives. So, what better way to reassure them of that, through the experiences of others who have already benefited and experienced the results from what you offer?

Customer success stories build trust and credibility. They create a narrative that potential customers can see themselves as part of. They allow people to picture their own successes and visualise how your product or service can solve their problems, meet their needs, or make their lives easier in some way. It's relatable, it's tangible, and it's incredibly persuasive.

How to Collect Customer Success Stories

To emphasise customer success stories, you first need to gather them in. This is all about reaching out, connecting with your customers, and asking them to share their experiences.

Try this:

> Ask for Testimonials: Sometimes, all you have to do is ask. After a customer has had a positive experience with one of your products or service offerings, reach out and ask if they would be willing to give a testimonial. Make it easy for them. Offer to send a few guiding questions, or suggest they share their thoughts in a way that's most comfortable for them. This could be an email, a video, or a social media shout-out. Post them to your website as *'What people are saying...'*
>
> Share Case Studies: Case studies are a more in-depth look at how your product or service has made a difference to the lives of your customers. Identify the customers who have seen significant beneficial results and work with them to craft a detailed story of their experiences. From the challenges they faced, which

brought them to you in the first place, to how they put your product or service into practice, to the outcomes they achieved. A well-crafted case study highlights successes and also provides a roadmap to real-life benefits and actual results others can easily follow.

Encourage Reviews: Online reviews are a form of success story that have the potential for huge impact. Encourage your customers to leave reviews on Google, Trust Pilot, Amazon or trade/industry-specific sites.

Make it easy for them to do so. Send a follow-up email after their purchase with a direct link to where they can leave a review. And remember to engage with these reviews.

Thank your customers for their feedback. Showcase positive ones across all your marketing channels. ALWAYS respond to any less-than-positive reviews with a clear remedy of how you are going to resolve the posters issue going forward. Never argue.

Where to Share Success Stories

Once you've collected success stories, it's time for you to share them far and wide. Don't let them merely lurk in a dusty corner of your website. They should be upfront and centre stage, helping to tell the story of your products or services through the voices of those who have used and experienced them at first-hand, and enjoyed positive results.

Your Website: Dedicate a section of your website to customer success stories. This could be a testimonials (w*hat people are saying*) page, a blog series featuring in-depth case studies, or even a rotating highlight on your homepage. Make sure the stories are easy to find and navigate. Potential customers should be able to quickly see how others have benefited from what you offer.

Social Media: Social media is a perfect place to share customer success stories It's where conversations are already going on. Share quotes, snippets, or full stories across your accounts. Use visuals – customer photos, infographics, or short videos – to make the stories more engaging. Tag the customers in (with their permission) to add authenticity and also encourage them to share the post within their own networks.

Email Marketing: Your email subscriber list is made up of people who are already interested in, or bought-into, what you do – making it the perfect medium for customer success stories. Include the stories in your regular newsletters, or create a dedicated email series highlighting several success stories over time. Position them as *inspirational content* – something your subscribers can look forward to and gain information from.

How to Make Success Stories Really Shine

Collecting and sharing customer success stories is great, but to make them really shine, you need to present them in a way that resonates well with your audience.

Here's how to do just that:

Focus on the Transformation: The heart of any great success story is the transformation. It's not only about the 'before' and 'after', it's also about the journey in between. What challenges did the customer face before they found your solution? How did your product or service help them overcome these challenges? And what precisely is different for them now? Highlighting the transformation makes the story relatable and shows potential customers what is realistically possible for them to achieve also.

Use the Customer's Own Voice: Let your customers tell their story in their own words as much as possible. By all means correct any spelling mistakes, nothing more. Authenticity is key here. There is nothing more authentic than a customer sharing their experience in their own words and in a way that feels natural to them. This could be a direct quote, a video, or a social media post. Using the customer's own words adds credibility and makes the story real. Plus, of course, eminently believable.

Highlight Specific Results: Wherever possible, include specific, measurable, actual results in the success stories. Numbers are incredibly persuasive. Did your product help a customer increase their profits by 20%? Did it save them 5 hours of time every week? How much did it improve their customer satisfaction scores? Specific results make the success story more convincing, because they are real-life, actual results.

Add Visuals: A picture is worth a thousand words, right? Well, in the world of marketing, a picture paired with a customer success story is worth even more. Include photos, charts, videos that help illustrate the customer's journey and results. Visuals make the story much more engaging and help potential customers envision their own success.

The Impact of Customer Success Stories

When you emphasise success stories, you're not just sharing feel-good anecdotes – you are building a bridge of trust between your business and potential customers. These stories are living proof that you consistently deliver on your promises; that you've helped others achieve their goals; and that you can do the same for them.

Builds Trust: In times of uncertainty, trust in a supplier is more valuable than ever. Prospective customers need to feel confident they are making the *right* decision.

Nothing builds confidence like hearing about the positive experiences of others.

Encourages Action: Customer success stories inspire action. When potential customers see how others have succeeded with your product or service, they are more likely to take the next step towards a purchase. They are highly motivated as they can appreciate the value, see the results and the realistic probability of their own success.

Creates Loyalty: Sharing success stories also strengthens your relationships with existing customers. It amply demonstrates that you are proud of their achievements; that you value their experiences; and you are invested in their ongoing success. This form of recognition and appreciation often turns already satisfied customers into staunch advocates.

Summary

Emphasising customer success stories is nothing about blowing your own trumpet, it's about giving real-life proof of the value you bring to the table. It's about giving potential customers the reassurance they need to move forward towards a purchase, confident in the knowledge they are making the right decision for them.

Collect those stories, share them far and wide, allow your customers' successes to speak for themselves. These are your best ambassadors.

BONUS CHAPTER 3

Simplify Your Customers' Experiences

When times get tough, simplicity becomes a sanctuary. People are juggling a lot of stuff in their daily lives during these times. Be that financial worries; time constraints; or the general stresses and strains that come with modern-day living, plus the high cost of living we're seeing these days.

The last thing people want is to be bogged down by a complicated purchasing process. What people crave is ease, clarity, and a straightforward path to getting what they need, or want, easily.

This is where you come in.

The Importance of Simplicity

In a world full of noise and distractions, a simple, clear customer experience is like a breath of fresh air. It's about reducing friction at every touchpoint – making sure your customers can find what they are looking for, understand the options, and complete the purchase with minimal effort. When you simplify their experience, you are making it easier for them to buy from you – you are showing you value their time.

Simplicity makes things easy, and builds confidence and trust. When your customers can navigate your website easily and effortlessly; find the information they need quickly, and make a purchase without jumping through hoop after hoop. It creates a seamless, positive experience. In difficult times, this can be the difference between a lost sale – or a one-time buyer – and a fully satisfied returning customer.

Simplify the Customer Experience

Streamline the Sales Process: Take a close look at your sales process from start to finish. Where are the sticking points? Are there any unnecessary steps that could be taken out? The aim here is to make it as easy as possible for your customers to go from browsing to buying. This means clear product descriptions; easy-to-find pricing information; and a checkout process that doesn't feel like climbing a sheer rock face.

Make Your Website Easy to Navigate: Your website is often the first place people interact with your business, so it needs to be as user-friendly as possible. Think about the customer journey – how can you make it intuitive and straightforward? Simplify the menu structure, use clear labels, and ensure the important information (such as contact details and pricing) is easy to find. Don't forget about smartphone users. A responsive, mobile-friendly design is absolutely crucial.

Clear Call To Action: When it comes to guiding your customers through the buying process, a clear call to action (CTA) is your best friend. Each page of your website should have a clear, singular focus, whether that's encouraging customers to learn more, sign up for your newsletter, or make a purchase. Use strong, action-oriented language in your CTA, and make sure it stands out visually, so there is no confusion about what the next step is.

Reduce the Number of Steps to Purchase: Every extra step in the purchasing process is an opportunity for customers to drop off. Simplify the checkout process by removing any unnecessary fields or steps. If possible, offer a guest checkout option so customers don't have to create an account to make a purchase. Also consider integrating payment methods that allow for quick, one-click transactions, like PayPal or digital wallets.

Bringing It All Together

Now, let's think about how all these elements work together to create a simplified, customer-centric experience. When your sales process is streamlined, your website is easy to navigate, and your CTA is clear, you are removing all obstacles that can make buying feel like a chore.

Here's the magic...

When customers discover it's really easy to do business with you, they are far more likely to return and become repeat customers. They will remember the positive experience they had with you previously and, in a world full of complicated processes and unclear options, they will gravitate towards the business that makes their lives a little easier and much more comfortable... yes, that's you.

The Ripple Effect

Simplicity in life has a way of creating a ripple effect. When you simplify your customer's experience, you are making things easier for them, which in turn makes things easier for your business. Fewer steps mean fewer opportunities for errors. Clearer navigation means fewer customer service inquiries. More straightforward options means less confusion and higher conversion rates.

Moreover, a simplified customer experience will most certainly enhance your reputation. Customers will talk about you. When they rave about how easy it is to buy from you; how straightforward the experience is; how seamless the checkout process feels – the word will spread. This is the kind of buzz you want, especially in times when *every* sale counts.

Summary

Consider simplifying the experience your customer has of your business overall, as a personal commitment from you to your customers. You are saying, *'We see you... we get it... we are here to make your life just that little bit easier for you'.* It's about creating a frictionless path from initial interest to final purchase, and doing it in a way that feels natural, simple, and intuitive.

So, take a step back, look at the path your customer faces from initial interest to final checkout. Ask yourself this, *'where can I make things easier, simpler, more straightforward?'* In this complicated world, simplicity isn't a *'nice-to-have'* – it's a *necessity* and key to building trust, encouraging loyalty, and making your business a place where customers want to return to, again and again.

What Now?

What determines whether you business will grow in tough times, by the fast pace you really want it to? How will you go beyond scratching around, barely surviving, to move on to skyrocket you profits to greater heights? Well, it's quite simply...

ACTION!

It's a cold hard fact. The businesses that achieve rapid growth – over a short period of time – do so because they are steadfastly *action-oriented*. They systematically and relentlessly apply powerful, effective marketing strategies that make quantum growth *predictable*.

My greatest wish now is that you will take what I have laid out in this book and apply it to your business. You *can* build the business of your dreams. Go now and build wealth and lasting fortune. Live the life of personal and financial riches that are yours for the taking.

One more thing. Realise this, nothing can stop you – other than you. Smash any misconceptions you may have about your worthiness, or your ability to massively succeed. You *can* achieve any business result you put your mind to when – and as soon as – you adopt and apply what I have shown you in this book.

The foundations of your success are contained in these pages. Apply them now and get ready to receive and accept abundant results. You deserve it.

I wish you all the very best in everything you do.

David Madely

Before you go…

If you get a moment, would you please leave a review of this book on Amazon? Obviously, I'm only human and would love for you to leave a glowing one – however, what I *really* care about is that you're honest and truthful.

If you didn't like the book, please say so and the reason why. I greatly value all feedback. If there's something you think could be better, by all means include that in your review. Similarly, if you enjoyed the book and learned something from it, please let me know also.

Thank you.

davidmadely.com

Printed in Great Britain
by Amazon

49634938R00119